Public Theology

First Fruits Press
The Academic Open Press of Asbury Theological Seminary
204 N. Lexington Ave., Wilmore, KY 40390
859-858-2236
first.fruits@asburyseminary.edu
asbury.to/firstfruits

Working Papers of the American Society of Missiology

Volume 3

——— ASM ———

American Society of Missiology

Public Theology

Edited by
Robert A. Danielson

William L. Selvidge

First Fruits Press
The Academic Open Press of Asbury Theological Seminary
204 N. Lexington Ave., Wilmore, KY 40390
859-858-2236
first.fruits@asburyseminary.edu
asbury.to/firstfruits

Public Theology
Edited by Robert A. Danielson and William L. Selvidge

First Fruits Press, ©2017
Digital version at http://place.asburyseminary.edu/academicbooks/16/

ISBN: 9781621716679 (print), 9781621716686 (digital), 9781621716693 (kindle)

For all other uses, contact:

First Fruits Press
B.L. Fisher Library
Asbury Theological Seminary
204 N. Lexington Ave.
Wilmore, KY 40390
http://place.asburyseminary.edu/firstfruits

American Society of Missiology (2016 : Wheaton, Illinois)
  Public Theology / American Society of Missiology; edited by Robert A. Danielson, William L. Selvidge. -- Wilmore, Kentucky: First Fruits Press, ©2017.
        xiv, 107 pages : illustrations; 21 cm. – (Working Papers of the American Society of Missiology; Volume III)
        Includes bibliographical references
        ISBN - 13: 9781621716679 (pbk.)
        1. Missions--Theory--Congresses. 2. Christianity and culture--Congresses. 3. Communication--Religious aspects--Christianity--Congresses. I. Title. II. Danielson, Robert A. (Robert Alden), 1969- III. Selvidge, William L..
BV2000.W674 Vol. 3

Cover design by Jon Ramsay

Table of Contents

Introduction

ROBERT DANIELSON

In 2016 the American Society of Missiology took as its primary theme, the topic of Public Theology, which examines how Christians live out their faith in the world that exists beyond the front door of our churches. This topic can encompass social action programs, political activities of the church, or mission activities that take the church to the people instead of expecting people to come to the church. It can be a little thing like putting on a public picnic in a local park to help the neighbors get to know the people in the church, or can be something big like a concerted effort by several denominations working together to confront the issue of sex trafficking through public protest and speaking at congressional hearings. The point is that the activity takes place in public spaces and is used to help the church make itself known and heard by a broader audience.

This volume of the working papers includes a fascinating range of cases where Christians moved into the public square to influence it. Takanori Inoue begins this discussion by examining how early Christians influenced the Roman Empire through their radical treatment of the poor in that society. Robert Danielson presents a case from mission history through examining a living example of Nahuat plays developed by Spanish missionaries in the early days of the Spanish conquest of the Aztec and Mayan worlds. Ronald Bartholomew examines the history of public engagement in the Church of Jesus Christ of Latter-Day Saints, which took them from being a very marginalized faith to developing a widely recognized public face through its mission program, the Mormon Tabernacle Choir, and other events over time. Grant Miller and Reuben Lang'at explore how social media and globalization have transformed the way the church operates in Kenya and Tanzania, in both positive and negative ways. Catholic scholar, Joanne Blaney, builds on her years of experience in Brazil and through case studies to examine how mission can be involved in building peace and restorative justice in areas affected by poverty and violence. Finally Bob Rice delves into the case of Rwanda, where the powerful East African Revival ultimately gave way to genocide. He looks at the role of the church in the history of Rwanda and explores its failure to respond to ethnic violence in the larger society.

In this work, we are in the second year of a new endeavor of the American Society of Missiology. During annual meetings, many professionals, practitioners, and students present informative papers in a variety of different areas. Often these papers are works in progress, not quite ready for publication, or are ideas looking for professional feedback. Sometimes these papers are just areas expressing the many side interests of the presenters. In most of these cases, these works will not be published as formal articles in *Missiology: An International Review* or other academic journals, but they still represent excellent ideas and works in progress that can stimulate the missiological community. To keep these ideas alive and active, the ASM decided to launch a series of volumes entitled "working papers." These papers have been presented at the annual meeting and the authors have polished them based on feedback received at the annual meeting, however these papers have not been peer-reviewed and should still be read in that light. They represent current ongoing academic thinking by current and rising missiologists and are presented here to encourage ongoing academic debate and critical thinking in the field of missiology.

The Early Church's Approach to the Poor in Society and Its Significance to the Church's Social Engagement Today

TAKANORI INOUE
PHD STUDENT AT ASBURY THEOLOGICAL SEMINARY

DOI: 10.7252/Paper. 000074

This paper focuses on the early Christian's[1] approach to the poor and reviews how their approach to the poor influenced the society and made differences there. The early Christian practice to the poor was very attractive to help the people in the society. First, this paper briefly grasps the economic situation in the early Roman Empire and the expansion of Christian population in the empire. Second, this paper reviews the theological background of the Christian practice for the poor and their typical practices in the society, especially in the urban environment and at the time of disasters. Then, this paper attempts to articulate the significant points for Christian social engagement today.

1. ECONOMIC SITUATION IN THE EARLY ROMAN EMPIRE

The Roman Empire maintained its domination of the Mediterranean world through judicial institutions, legislative systems, property ownership, control of labor, and brute force. Like most societies, the empire developed mechanisms for maintaining multifaceted inequality and promoted justifications that made the inequity seem normal or at least inevitable.[2]

In the economic facets of the Roman system of inequality, there are three fundamental ideas to keep in mind. First, the Roman imperial economy was pre-industrial. The vast majority of people lived in rural areas or in small towns, with only about ten to fifteen percent of the population in big cities of ten thousand people or more. This means that most of the population worked in agriculture (about eighty to ninety percent) and that large-scale commercial or manufacturing activity was rare.[3]

Second, there was no middle class in the Roman Empire. Since the economy was mainly agricultural, wealth was based on the ownership of land. Most land was controlled by a limited number of wealthy, elite families. These families earned rent

---

1   In this paper the early church and early Christians mean that the churches and Christians were in the period between after the primitive church in Jerusalem and before the establishment of Christendom.

2   Peter Garnsey and Richard Saller, *The Roman Empire: Economy, Society, and Culture* (Berkeley: University of California Press, 1987), 125.

3   Steven J. Friesen, "Injustice or God's Will?: Early Christian Explanations of Poverty," in *Wealth and Poverty in Early Church and Society*, edited by Susan R. Holman (Grand Rapids: Baker Academic, 2008), 19.

and produce from the farmers and/or slaves who actually worked at the land. With their wealth and status, these families were able to control regional governance, which allowed them to earn profit from taxation and from governmental policies. These families also controlled the public religion.[4]

Third, inequality was widespread both in rural and urban areas. Friesen developed a poverty scale that provides seven categories for describing economic resources as seen below. Super-wealthy elites (categories 1–3) made up less than three percent of the total imperial population. On the other hand, ninety percent of the total population was near and under subsistence level.

Poverty Scale (PS) for a Large City in the Roman Empire[5]

Percent of Population	Poverty Scale Categories
0.04%	**PS1. Imperial elites**: imperial dynasty, Roman senatorial families, a few retainers, local royalty, a few freed persons.
1%	**PS 2. Regional or provincial elites**: equestrian families, provincial officials, some retainers, some decurial families, some freed persons, some retired military officers.
1.76%	**PS 3. Municipal elites**: most decurial families, wealthy men and women who do not hold offices, some freed persons, some retainers, some veterans, some merchants.
7%	**PS 4. Moderate surplus resources**: some merchants, some traders, some freed persons, some artisans, and military veterans
22%	**PS 5. Stable near subsistence level**: many merchants and traders, regular wage earners, artisans, large shop owners, freed persons, some farm families.

---

4   Ibid.
5   Ibid., 20. In rural areas poverty was even worse.

| 40% | **PS 6. At subsistence level**: small farm families, laborers, artisans, wage earners, most merchants and traders, small shop owners. |
| 28% | **PS 7. Below subsistence level**: some farm families, unattached widows, orphans, beggars, disabled, unskilled day laborers, prisoners. |

Annual Income Needed For a Family of Four[6]

For wealth in Rome (PS 3)	25,000 – 150,000 denarii
For modest prosperity in Rome (PS 4)	5,000 denarii
For subsistence in Rome (PS 5-6)	900 – 1,000 denarii
For subsistence in a city (PS 5-6)	600 – 700 denarii
For subsistence in the country (PS 5-6)	250 – 300 denarii

In the early Roman Empire financial resources were likely the most influential factor in determining one's place in the social economy. Other factors were gender, ethnicity, family lineage (common or noble), legal status (slave, freed, or freeborn), occupation, and education. Patronage relationships were important in one's economic survival because a patron gave one access to restricted resources that were unavailable. In times of crisis, a patron could mean the difference between life and death.[7]

2. GROWING CHRISTIAN POPULATION AND THE ATTRACTIONS

As the Book of Acts in the New Testament reported, in the early Roman Empire period Christianity was rapidly growing. Although it is difficult to

---

6   Ibid. Categories from the poverty scale are in parentheses.

7   For further discussion of these issues, see Anthony J. Blasi, Jean Duhaime, and Paul-André Turcotte, eds., *Handbook of Early Christianity: Social Science Approaches* (Walnut Creek: AltaMira, 2002).

articulate the number of Christians in this Early Church, it is estimated as seen below that there were a thousand Christians in the year 40, about 7,500 in the year 100, about 217,000 in the year 200, and six million Christians at the beginning of the fourth century. Christianity grew at the rate of forty percent per decade. About ten percent of the empire's population was Christian by the time of Constantine.[8]

Christian Growth Projected at Forty Percent per Decade[9]

Year	Number of Christians	Percent of Population
40	1,000	0.0017
50	1,400	0.0023
100	7,530	0.0126
150	40,490	0.07
200	217,795	0.36
250	1,171,356	1.9
300	6,299,832	10.5
350	33,882,008	56.5

This growth is impressive if we consider the social situation of the early Christians. Despite the scorn of the powerful and persecutions, the early Christian movement was growing. This implies something was deeply attractive to the society.

There are three major facets by which the early church attracted people.[10] First, Christians' self-identity as "resident aliens" (*paroikoi*) was unique in the unsettled world of late antiquity. This was a familiar legal term, which many Christians from the First Epistle of Peter to the early centuries used to express their sense of identification with cultures in which they embodied new approaches and insights.[11] Christians brought news that was new for the people and new perspectives and possibilities. At the same time, they expressed these in a symbolic and social language that was familiar and that addressed people's questions and

---

8   Rodney Stark, *The Rise of Christianity: A Sociologist Reconsiders History* (Princeton: Princeton University Press, 1996), 6.

9   Stark, *The Rise of Christianity*, 7. Based on an estimated population of sixty million.

10   Alan Kreider, *The Change of Conversion and the Origin of Christendom* (Harrisburg, PA: Trinity Press International, 1999), 15-20.

11   Ibid., 15.

struggles. Christian worship likely helped the early Christians to shape their lives, character, and communities, so that they would be intriguingly vital.

Second, Christian beliefs and power were attractive.[12] Christian belief was an important element in early Christian growth because Christ had conquered death so that Christians need not to fear death, for they will rise from it.[13] This belief encouraged them to withstand persecution. Divine power among the early Christians also attracted people. As Tertullian put it, the Christians were in "touch with the miraculous."[14] People who possessed gifts of healing were an accepted part of many Christian communities.[15] Exorcism likely took a more important role. For people, the world was contested terrain in which demons persisted in exercising their power and many people felt themselves to be oppressed by spiritual forces and longed for liberation.[16] As a result, liberation from demonic power was one of the chief benefits that the churches could offer to potential converts.[17]

Third, the Christians' behavior attracted people.[18] The behavior of the Christians was the product of careful pre-baptismal catechizing by church leaders who attempted to apply the teaching of Christ to the lives of their congregation.[19] Also, the early Christians' self-identity as "resident aliens" developed the Christians' lifestyle, and their social reality spread and transcended the Roman Empire.[20] Christian congregations expressed their reality by corresponding with other churches, by providing hospitality to travelers, and by supporting fellow Christians who were prisoners.[21] The early Christian communities were marked by economic sharing and social care for the poor.[22] The communities consisted of various ranges of social classes and were bound by love and rite into a brotherhood/sisterhood.

---

12   Ibid., 16.

13   Ibid.

14   Ibid.

15   Geoffrey J. Cuming ed., *Hippolytus: A Text for Students*, Second edition (Bramcote, Nottingham: Grove Books, 1987), 14. Cited in Kreider, 16.

16   Kreider, 17.

17   Everett Ferguson, *Demonology of the Early Christian World* (New York: Edwin Mellen Press, 1984), 129. Irenaeus mentioned: people who have been delivered by acts of miraculous power frequently both believe and join themselves to the church. Cited in Kreider, 17.

18   Kreider, 17.

19   Kreider, 18.

20   Kreider, 18-19.

21   Kreider, 19.

22   Ibid.

3. The Early Christian Approach to the Poor

As seen above, despite persecution and disadvantages in their social situation, the Christian population was growing because the early Church attracted people in the early Roman Empire. The greatest attractions were Christians' practices and behaviors. An essential part of Christian communities depended on their willingness to aid those in need and on the teachings of the Christian church about the right use of material goods. In this section, this paper reviews the early Christians' teachings and their practices in detail.

3-1 The Early Christian Teaching of the Poor

The early Christians lived as "resident aliens" in the early Roman Empire. This self-identity reflected their teachings. At the first century, the author of the *Didache* repeated the scriptural teachings that people are faced with two options: they can choose the way of life or way of death. The Christians who choose the way of life must first love God, and then his neighbor as themselves. In practice, if one has material possessions, one must freely give to those who are in need: "Give to anyone that asks, without looking for any repayment, for it is the Father's pleasure that we should share his gracious bounty with all men."[23] The point is not only that the things of earth belong to God, but also that he has made them available for use. Sharing material goods is to replace possessing the goods as a value for Christians.

A work of the early second century, Hermas, an Apostolic Father argues in his work *Shepherd of Hermas* how the rich can be saved and provides the main requirement to the rich – helping the poor. *Shepherd of Hermas* states: "assist widows, visit orphans and the poor, ransom God's servants, show hospitality, help oppressed debtors in their need."[24] Hermas insists that, since Christians are strangers in a strange land and not permanent residents of this world, they should not settle in like colonists and not increase wealthist for the sake of being rich. Their priorities should be, "instead of fields, purchase afflicted souls, as each is able.

---

23 *Didache*, 1.1, 5. Quoted in William J. Walsh and John P. Langan, "Patristic Social Consciousness: The Church and the Poor," in *The Faith That Does Justice: Examining the Christian Sources for Social Change*, edited by John C. Haughey (New York: Paulist Press, 1977), 114.

24 *Mandates* 8:10. Quoted in Walsh and Langan, 115.

And visit widows and orphans, and do not neglect them. Spend your wealth and all your possessions on such fields and houses which you received from God. For the Master made you rich for this purpose that you might perform these ministries for him."[25]

These theological concepts - love, sharing our goods, the right use of wealth, God as the Creator and the Provider of the material world – were passed to later Christians – e.g. Irenaeus of Lyons, Clement of Alexandria, Origen, Tertullian, Cyprian of Carthage, Lactantius.[26] The early Christians' teaching was likely different from the teaching and practice of heresies. In the second century, Ignatius of Antioch characterized heretics as those who "have no regard for love; no care for the widow, or the orphan, or the oppressed; of the bond, or of the free; of the hungry, or of the thirsty."[27] Also, at the reign of Julian (360–363) – a pagan interlude in the empire after Constantine – Julian attempted to revive paganism by using the philanthropic practices of the despised Christians to develop charitable institutions. He wrote a letter to a pagan priest:

> We ought then to share our money with all men, but more generously with the good, and with the helpless and poor so as to suffice for their need. And I will assert, even though it be paradoxical to say so, that it would be a pious act to share our clothes and food even with the wicked. For it is to the humanity in a man that we give, and not to his moral character. Hence I think that even those who are shut up in prison have a right to the same sort of care, since this kind of philanthropy will not hinder justice.[28]

---

25   *Similitudes* 1. 8-9. Quoted in Everett Ferguson, *Early Christians Speak: Faith and Life in the First Three Centuries*, Third Edition (Abilene, TX: ACU Press, 1999), 205.

26   See Ferguson, *Early Christians Speak*, 203-206 and Justo L. González, *Faith and Wealth: A History of Early Christian Ideas on the Origin, Significance, and Use of Money* (New York, Harper & Row, 1990), 92-144.

27   *Ad Smyrnaeans*, 6.2. Quoted in González, 101.

28   *Epistles*, 290D-291A. Quoted in Binger A. Pearson, *The Emergence of the Christian Religion: Essays on Early Christianity* (Harrisburg, PA: Trinity Press International, 1997), 211.

As an example, Julian cited the Jews as well as Christians:

> It is disgraceful that, when no Jew ever had to beg, and the impious
> Galileans [Christians] support not only their own poor but ours as
> well, all men see that our people [pagans] lack aid from us.[29]

These references, both by a Christian and a pagan, are the fact that the
early Christian teaching was more or less practiced by the Christians in their
communities and the societies.

3-2 An Example of the Early Christian Practice to the Poor

How did the early Christians behave in a crisis, such as in severe epidemics?
Two great epidemics struck the Roman Empire – in 165–180 and in 251–266.
Mortality was high in many cities and rural areas. William H. McNeil estimated
that from a quarter to a third of the population perished during the former epidemic.
In the latter epidemic, at its height, five thousand people a day were reported to
have died in the city of Rome alone.[30]

In these epidemics, Christians offered an explanation and comfort when all
other faiths were called into question. As Cyprian, bishop of Carthage wrote in 251:

> Many of us are dying in this mortality, that is many of us are being
> freed from the world .... to the servant of God it is a salutary
> departure. ... the just are dying with the unjust, ... The just are called
> to refreshment, the unjust are carried off to torture; protection is
> more quickly given to the faithful; punishment to the faithless ....
> How suitable, how necessary it is that this plague and pestilence,
> ... searches out the justice of each and every one and examines
> the minds of the human race; whether the well care for the sick,
> whether relatives dutifully love their kinsman as they should,
> whether masters show compassion for their ailing slaves, whether
> physicians do not desert the afflicted . ... Although this mortality
> has contributed nothing else, it has especially accomplished this
> for Christians and servants of God, that we have begun gladly to
> seek martyrdom while we are learning not to fear death. These are

---

29   Ibid., 22. 430D. Quoted in Pearson, 211.
30   William H. McNeil, *Plagues and Peoples* (Garden City, NY: Doubleday, 1983), 131.

> trying exercises for us, not deaths; they give to the mind the glory
> of fortitude; by contempt of death they prepare for the crown.
> … [O]ur brethren who have been freed from the world by the
> summons of the Lord should not be mourned, since we know that
> they are not lost but sent before; that in departing they lead the
> way; that as travelers, as voyagers are wont to be, they should be
> given to pagans to censure us deservedly and justly, on the ground
> that we grieve for those who we say are living with God.[31]

Also Dionysius of Alexandria wrote to address his members: "Other people would not think this a time for festival, far from being a time of distress, it is a time of unimaginable joy."[32] Although the epidemics terrified the pagans, Christians almost welcomed them and accepted them as schooling and testing. Christian beliefs differed with pagan beliefs in their explanatory capacities. Christian beliefs made human history purposeful even in the face of what seemed mere caprice to pagans.[33] Moreover, Christian beliefs provided instructions for action.

During the second great epidemic, Dionysius wrote in an Easter letter around 260 that a substantial number of his presbyters, deacons, and laymen lost their lives while caring for others:

> Most of our brother Christians showed unbounded love and
> loyalty, never sparing themselves and thinking only of one another.
> Heedless of danger, they took charge of the sick, attending to their
> every need and ministering to them in Christ, and with them
> departed this life serenely happy …. Many, in nursing and curing
> others, transferred their death to themselves and died in their stead
> …. The best of our brothers lost their lives in this manner; a number
> of presbyters, deacons, and laymen winning high commendation
> so that death in this form, the result of great piety and strong faith,
> seems in every way the equal of martyrdom.[34]

---

31   *Mortality*, 15-20. Quoted in Mcneil, 136-137 and Stark, *The Rise of Christianity*, 81.
32   *Festival Letters*, quoted in Stark, *The Rise of Christianity*, 82.
33   Rodney Stark, "Antioch As the Social Situation for Matthew's Gospel," in *Social History of the Matthean Community: Cross-Disciplinary Approaches*, edited by David L. Bulch (Minneapolis: Fortress Press, 1991), 203.
34   Stark, *The Rise of Christianity*, 82.

He also described how the pagans responded:

> The heathen behaved in the very opposite way. At the first onset of the disease, they pushed the sufferers away and fled from their dearest, throwing them into the roads before they were dead and treated unburied corpses as dirt, hoping thereby to avert the spread and contagion of the fatal disease; but do what they might, they found it difficult to escape.[35]

If we are to assess Dionysius' claims, it must be demonstrated that the Christians actually did minister to the sick while the pagans mostly did not. Large numbers of people died not directly from the disease, but from dehydration and lack of calories because they became too weak to obtain food and liquids. Modern medical experts estimate that conscientious nursing without any medications could cut the mortality rate by two-thirds or even more.[36] Therefore, if the Christians nursed the sick, they would have had a far lower mortality rate than pagans.

As Stark argues, Christians revitalized life in Greco-Roman cities by providing new norms and new kinds of social relationships able to cope with many urgent urban problems. To cities filled with the homeless, impoverished, and strangers, Christians offered an immediate basis for attachments. To cities filled with orphans and widows, Christians provided a new and expanded sense of family. To cities torn by violent ethnic strife, Christians offered a new basis for social solidarity. And to cities faced with epidemic, fires and earthquakes, Christians offered effective nursing services.[37] Thus, the early Christians ministered as a transformative movement that arose in response to the misery, chaos, fear and brutality of life in the Roman Empire.

---

35   Ibid. This is similar with what Thucydides reported about the great epidemic that struck Athens in 431 B.C.E: "[The Victims] died with no one to look after them; indeed there were many houses in which all the inhabitants perished through lack of any attention. ... The bodies of the dying were heaped one on top of the other, and half dead creatures could be seen staggering about in the streets or flocking around the fountains in their desire for water. ... As for the gods, it seemed to be the same thing whether one worshiped them or not, when one saw the good and the bad dying indiscriminately." Quoted in Stark, "Antioch As the Social Situation for Matthew's Gospel," 202.

36   Stark, "Antioch As the Social Situation for Matthew's Gospel," 203.

37   Stark, The Rise of Christianity, 161.

4. Significance of the Early Church's Approach for Today

As seen above, the early Roman Empire had an unequal economic system and ninety percent of the total population was near an under subsistence level. Despite the scorn of the powerful and persecutions, the early Christian movement was growing. Three major facets that attracted people to Christianity were the early Christians' self-identity as "resident aliens," Christian beliefs and spiritual power, and the Christians' behavior. In their approach to the poor, the early Christians succeeded in its theological concepts – love, sharing goods, the right use of wealth, God as the Creator and Provider of the material world – from generation to generation. Moreover, they actually ministered to the poor through nursing and caring for them. This early church movement was transformative and revitalized life in the empire.

This early church's approach to the poor in society provides at least five fundamental theological concepts for Christian social engagement today. First, God's (Christ's) reign that is against the power of the world is clearly shown. They had a strong self-identity as "resident aliens" that was unique in the unsettled world of late antiquity and brought new perspectives and possibilities in the reign of God. Also, the divine power shown among the early Christians – such as healing and exorcism represents God's reign and Christ's rule over all things.

Justice is another significant concept – such as their view of God and the practice of sharing. As *Didache* teaches, the things of the earth belong to God and God has made them available for use. This notion – God as the Creator and the Provider of the material world – encourages the early Christians to share their material goods with those in need. Then sharing goods became a value and ministry for them. As Hermas states, the early rich Christians were encouraged to redistribute their wealth and possessions to the vulnerable in the severely imbalanced social economy of the Roman Empire.

Love is linked with the love of God and the love of neighbor. The early Christians' lifestyle shows their love by providing hospitality to travelers, supporting imprisoned Christians, and caring for the poor. Their communities – consisting of various ranges of social classes – were bound by love and rite into a brotherhood/sisterhood. As seen in their teachings, the early Christians chose this way of life and so they first loved God and then their neighbors as themselves.

In practice, they freely gave to those who were in need without looking for any repayment, because it is God's pleasure that they should share his generosity with all people. Their love spread even to pagans and expanded to the point of loosing their lives while they cared for others.

Well-being is another concept seen in the early church. Since the early Christians offered effective nursing service when they faced epidemics, fires, and earthquakes, they had a far lower mortality rate than others. This early Christian ministry was a transformative movement that arose in response to the misery, chaos, fear, and brutality of life in their social contexts.

Friendship and companionship is also a major characteristic. The early Christians revitalized life in Greco-Roman cities by providing new norms and new kinds of social relationships that enabled them to cope with many urgent urban problems. They offered an immediate basis for attachment and brought a new and expanded view of family to society that was filled with the homeless and impoverished, and widows and orphans. In this sense, the early Christians provided a new basis for social solidarity.

In the early church's practices, there are at least three significant points for our social engagement today. First, it is important to keep our Christian identity as a "resident alien" steady. The Church has experienced a paradigm shift – from modernism to post-modernism. While the western churches have confronted post-Christendom, the churches in the third-world seem to find their identities in their context. At this point, a steady identity as "resident aliens" holds and strengthens the church in the complexity of values and the diversity of the world. In cross-cultural ministry and missions to the unreached areas where non-Christian religions dominate, it is crucial to hold this identity steady. Also, as "resident aliens," Christians could advocate and incarnate approaches to living that are both novel and comprehensive.

The early Christians integrated teaching/theology into practice – it is more holistic and there is no tension and separation between the word and the deed. In the early Roman Empire, the Christians actually practiced their beliefs. Therefore, their practice was so influential that even pagans realized what the Christians were doing, especially at the time of crisis – i.e. they cared for the poor, nursed the sick, and so on. Thus Julian, a pagan emperor, attempted to imitate the Christian practices for reviving paganism. For both of the western churches and the third-world churches it is significant to practice their beliefs. This does not mean that the churches are involved in ministry to show off their own behaviors. Christians today have to dedicate themselves more to God and others and live out their belief.

The early Christians' behavior and practice were done in their daily life. They formed communities with their brothers and sisters in love and expressed their reality through economic sharing/giving and care for the poor. They practiced their gifts from God to meet people's needs. In this sense, their behavior and practice were not projects. They served where they were in their daily life. This attracted people in the Roman Empire. Also, there was no dichotomy between the clergy and laity, which the church has since confronted for long periods. By building networks in the love of God and ministering to their neighbors in need, the church (and each Christian) could encourage and support each other, and serve spiritually and physically in various parts of the society where each Christian lives. Thus more people would come to realize the love of God.

BIBLIOGRAPHY

Blasi, Anthony J., Jean Duhaime and Paul-André Turcotte, eds.
    2002 *Handbook of Early Christianity: Social Science Approaches.* Walnut Creek, CA: AltaMira.

Brown, Peter
    2002 *Poverty and Leadership in the Later Roman Empire.* Hanover, NH: University Press of New England, 2002.

Cuming, Geoffrey J., ed.
    1987 *Hippolytus: A Text for Students.* 2nd ed. Bramcote, Nottingham, UK: Grove Books, 1987.

Dunn, Geoffrey D.
    2006 "Cyprian's Care for the Poor: The Evidence of *De Opere et Eleemosynis.*" *Studia Patristica* 42: 363-368.

Ferguson, Everett
    1984 *Demonology of the Early Christian World.* New York: Edwin Mellen Press.

    1999 *Early Christians Speak: Faith and Life in the First Three Centuries.* 3rd ed. Abilene, TX: ACU Press, 1999.

Friesen, Steven J.
    2008 "Injustice or God's Will?: Early Christian Explanations of Poverty." In *Wealth and Poverty in Early Church and Society*, edited by Susan R. Holman, 17-36. Grand Rapids, MI: Baker Academic.

Garnsey, Peter, and Richard Saller.
    1987 *The Roman Empire: Economy, Society, and Culture.* Berkeley, CA: University of California Press.

González, Justo L.
    1990 *Faith and Wealth: A History of Early Christian Ideas on the Origin, Significance, and Use of Money.* New York, Harper & Row.

Hinson, E. Glenn
1996   *The Early Church: Origins to the Dawn of the Middle Ages.* Nashville: Abingdon Press, 1996.

Hoornaert, Eduardo
1988   *The Memory of the Christian People.* Translated by Robert R. Barr Maryknoll, NY: Orbis Books.

Kreider, Alan
1996   *The Change of Conversion and the Origin of Christendom.* Harrisburg, PA: Trinity Press International.

Marsden, George
1980   *Fundamentalism and American Culture.* Oxford: Oxford University Press.

McNeil, William H.
1983   *Plagues and Peoples* (Garden City, NY: Doubleday.

Neil, Stephen
1986   *A History of Christian Mission.* 2nd ed. New York: Penguin Books, 1986.

Olasky, Marvin N.
1992   *The Tragedy of American Compassion.* Wheaton, IL: Crossway.

Pearson, Binger A.
1997   *The Emergence of the Christian Religion: Essays on Early Christianity* Harrisburg, PA: Trinity Press International.

Robert, Dana L.
2009   *Christian Mission: How Christianity Became a World Religion* Malden, MA: Wiley-Blackwell.

Shaw, Brent D.
2002   "Loving the Poor." *New York Review* 49, no. 18 (November 21, 2002): 42-45.

Stark, Rodney
1991   "Antioch As the Social Situation for Matthew's Gospel." In *Social History of the Matthean Community: Cross-Disciplinary Approaches*, edited by David L. Bulch, 189-210. Minneapolis, MN: Fortress Press.

1996 *The Rise of Christianity: A Sociologist Reconsiders History.* Princeton, NJ: Princeton University Press, 1996.

Walsh, William J., and John P. Langan.
1977 "Patristic Social Consciousness: The Church and the Poor." In *The Faith That Does Justice: Examining the Christian Sources for Social Change*, edited by John C. Haughey. New York: Paulist Press.

Winter, Bruce W.
1994 *Seek the Welfare of the City: Christians as Benefactors and Citizens* Grand Rapids, MI: William B. Eerdmans Publishing Company.

The Talcigüines of El Salvador:

A Contextual Example of Nahua Drama in the Public Square

Robert A. Danielson, Ph.D.

Asbury Theological Seminary

DOI: 10.7252/Paper. 000075

Abstract:

Anthropologist Louise M. Burkhart has spent decades studying the literary dramas of the Nahua speakers of 16th and 17th century Colonial Mexico. While many of these dramas illustrate the blending of Christianity with pre-Christian indigenous religion in Latin America, they have seldom been studied as early examples of contextualized Christianity or syncretism within early Spanish missions in Latin America.

These early Nahua dramas became elaborate performances that expressed indigenous understandings of Christian stories and theology. Burkhart notes that Spanish priests controlled Nahua drama through reviewing and approving the scripts, but also by keeping the performances out of the church buildings. This approach did not stop these contextualized dramas, but rather integrated them into traditional religious performances acted out in public spaces.

While many of these dramas exist now only as ancient scripts or recorded accounts, some modern remnants may still exist. One possibility is the Talcigüines of Texistepeque, El Salvador. Performed every Monday of Holy Week, this festival continues to combine Christian themes with indigenous symbols, moving from within the church to the literal public square. Developed for the Nahua speaking Pipil people of one of the oldest colonial parishes in El Salvador, this drama contains many of Burkhart's elements.

INTRODUCTION

On the Monday of Holy Week each year, a unique performance occurs in the small town of Texistepeque, in the western region of El Salvador in Central America. Masked figures dressed in red, called locally the Talcigüines, emerge from the local church of San Esteban and infest the public square adjacent to the church. Armed with whips, these figures attack the local population gathered in the square for a local fiesta. These attacks go on for the entire morning, until noon, when a figure representing Jesus Christ emerges from the church and battles and subdues the Talcigüines.

While this event is enjoyed by both the local population and visitors, it also presents an interesting possible remnant of early Spanish mission practice in Central America. This paper explores this event in more detail, especially in the light of historical studies of Nahua dramas to understand the origins and indigenous meanings behind this practice, where Jesus leaves the confines of the church to enter and save the public square.

NAHUA DRAMA AND EARLY SPANISH MISSIONS

In many ways, it is time we reexamined early Spanish missions in the field of missiology. Work has been coming out since the 1970s in other fields, particularly drama, music, and linguistics focused on the indigenous response to colonization in the Americas.[1] Unfortunately, many missiologists have not really picked up the torch to reevaluate such studies from what is often maligned as a dark time in missions. We often forget that early Spanish missions were the dawning of a new age in the Church that was not familiar with cross-cultural mission. While there were tragic mistakes and problems, made well known through works like *A Short Account of the Destruction of the Indies* by Dominican friar Bartolomé de las Casas, there were also new and innovative attempts at developing catechisms in the indigenous languages, training indigenous clergy, and innovative attempts at evangelization through drama, which are often underreported in the missiological literature. As linguists and art and music historians have begun to uncover documents in the

---

1   Cf. John F. Schaller, "Evangelization as Performance: Making Music, Telling Stories," *The Americas* 66(3): 305-310 (Jan. 2010).

voice of the original peoples of the Americas, it is time to reflect again on this time period in mission history.[2]

Anthropologist Louise M. Burkhart has done most of the historical academic work on Nahua dramas over a number of decades, where she has focused on collecting and documenting the written sources of these dramas, primarily in Mexico. She does not look at them through a missiological lens, but rather a literary or historical lens. It is interesting to note that drama as an evangelistic tool started quite early. Burkhart writes,

> The early Franciscan friars began staging Nahuatal plays as a strategy for evangelization. The first such performance on record is a dramatization of Judgment Day, with Christ meting out punishments on sinners who were unprepared for the world's end. Enacted in Tlatelolco in 1531 or 1533, this play so impressed the native audience that the event was recorded by Nahua chroniclers. The same or a similar play was performed in 1535 at San José de los Naturales in Tenochtitlan. The friars thought that the play led many people to accept Christianity. Drama became a standard tool of the missionary trade throughout the colony, with the other religious orders, even the Carmelite monks at San Sebastián, eventually following the Franciscans' example.[3]

She points out that pre-colonial religious ceremonies in Mexico were public events in which religious stories were dramatized, with sacrificial victims actually becoming the gods and being involved in processions while people participated in preparing food, decorating public spaces and watching the performance as well.[4] It is significant to point out her comments regarding how Nahua culture perceived the actor in a religious role from the pre-conquest period. She notes,

> That Nahuas conceived of the human being not as a firmly individualized personality but as a rather unstable assemblage of

2   Cf. Louise M. Burkart. *Before Guadalupe: The Virgin Mary in Colonial Nahuatl Literature.* Institute for Mesoamerican Studies Monograph 13. (Albany, NY: University at Albany) 2001. This work is a good example of how the indigenous voice can be heard again within a religious context.

3   Louise M. Burkhart, *Holy Wednesday: A Nahua Drama from Early Colonial Mexico.* (Philadelphia: University of Pennsylvania Press), 1996, pp. 42-43.

4   Louise M. Burkhart, ed. *Aztecs on Stage: Religious Theater in Colonial Mexico,* 2011, Norman, OK: University of Oklahoma Press, p. 5.

parts affected their conceptions of impersonation. Putting on the costume of a deity made that being manifest in one's own person. The regalia represented the god via metonymic substitution; the god's identity added itself to the aggregate of components that comprised the person. Both personae were fully present. This situation might be best expressed not as a state of being "not" and "not not" oneself, but rather as an equally liminal condition of being both oneself and another.[5]

As evidence of this state, even after the conquest, she points out to how indigenous believers would collect fake "blood" shed by the character playing Christ for its healing powers, or offer him incense or kisses, because the actor in part became Christ.[6]

At the same time, religious performance in Spain, from the Middle Ages was also popular, with biblical stories being conveyed in dramatic fashion through outside pageants at various festival occasions. It seems natural that the early Catholic missionaries would combine the religious pageantry they knew in Spain with local tradition in order to communicate the Gospel through indigenous symbols and language.

Burkhart[7] writes that Nahua dramas could be divided into two major categories: morality plays, and stories from the Bible. Stories from the Bible were more numerous, and of these, the largest numbers were designed as Passion plays to be performed at Easter time. Catholic priests would attempt to control the content of the plays by writing them out in the indigenous languages.[8] But at the same time, Catholic priests frequently relied on native speakers to help them with translation, so many of these dramas were true cross-cultural collaborations. In this type of transition, often the Catholic saints became mixed with the ideas of various traditional deities.

---

5   Louise M. Burkhart, *Holy Wednesday: A Nahua Drama from Early Colonial Mexico.* (Philadelphia: University of Pennsylvania Press), 1996, pp. 44.

6   Louise M. Burkhart, ed. *Aztecs on Stage: Religious Theater in Colonial Mexico,* 2011, Norman, OK: University of Oklahoma Press, p. 18-19.

7   Ibid., p. 7.

8   Of course translation has always been a complicated issue in terms of communicating religious ideas. For more on this from a Nahua perspective, see Louise M. Burkart, *The Slippery Earth: Nahua-Christian Moral Dialogue in Sixteenth-Century Mexico.* (Tucson, AZ: The University of Arizona Press) 1989.

In a political sense, the performance of a drama allowed the local community a place to celebrate their group identity and to bring in commerce to the local marketplace, as well as to produce an event with religious meaning. In terms of religious power, according to Burkhart, this accomplished some interesting side effects,

> Another reason for colonial authorities to be suspicious of Nahuatl drama lay in the very nature of theater. Even if priests scrutinized the scripts and checked to see that people recited their lines correctly, they were ceding power to the performers. Actors are themselves and their characters at the same time. Plays tell stories yet at the same time comment on the local setting, the place and people around the performance. Theater allowed Nahuas to become Jesus, Mary, saints, angels, devils, Jews, Romans, soldiers, priests, and every other sort of character, right in the centers of their own communities, while also remaining themselves- looking and talking like ordinary native people, one's friends and relations, not foreigners who spoke Nahuatl with Spanish accents, if they spoke it at all. Most statues and paintings in Nahua churches had European features, but the actors did not. The performance space- typically the churchyard, at the community's symbolic center- became Jerusalem, Bethlehem, Rome, heaven, hell. Cosmic events were made local; sacred powers, both helpful and harmful, were embodied in Nahua persons.[9]

As Burkhart goes on to mention, especially with Passion plays, the images of an indigenous Jesus being crucified by oppressive powers was most likely a very powerful symbol for indigenous people under the colonial oppression of the Spanish Empire. One way she notes that Catholic authorities tried to exert control over dramas was by banning them from the use of the church, but this of course encouraged the movement of such dramas into the public square even more,[10]

9   Louise M. Burkhart, ed. *Aztecs on Stage: Religious Theater in Colonial Mexico*, 2011, Norman, OK: University of Oklahoma Press, p.. 18.

10   It is important to recognize that the "church" as it was understood in this context was also different. An excellent diagram of the church can be seen in Diego Valadés' *Rhetorica Christiana* from 1579, with a good discussion of this found in Kenneth Mills and William Taylor's *Colonial Spanish America: A Documentary History*. Wilmington, DE: Scholarly Resources, Inc. 1998: 138-140. The church itself was only part of a larger area where baptisms, marriages, catechesis, and group instruction occurred more in a courtyard

with Passion plays sometimes even occurring in the local cemetery. Such dramas in Mexico were performed from 1533 to the late 1700s. While it is often assumed that the practice of these traditional dramas has died out, I believe it may still be possible to find remnants, such as the Talcigüines of El Salvador, which are still being performed.

Key aspects to note as we examine the Talcigüines of El Salvador as a form of Nahua drama are the following:

1. Nahua dramas often occur in Holy Week

2. Nahua drama typically takes place in the public square

3. Indigenous local performers play the key roles

4. The Nahuatl language or pantomime is used

5. Nahua dramas date back to the earliest period of Spanish mission

6. Nahua drama incorporates Nahua indigenous symbols

It is my hope to demonstrate in this paper, how the Talcigüines performance might be a surviving case of the Nahua dramas Burkhart records from ancient Mexico.

HISTORICAL CONTEXT OF THE TALCIGÜINES

One of the first points of concern will be to indicate how a Nahua performance from Mexico came to be performed in El Salvador. The indigenous people of western and central El Salvador are the Pipil people. Linguistic and archaeological evidence shows that they are the result of a migration of Nahuatl speaking peoples from Mexico along the coast of Guatemala between A.D. 700 and A.D. 1350.[11] In many regards the Pipil are more similar to the Aztec in terms of their deities and religious practices than their Mayan neighbors. While some aspects of their culture were borrowed from contact with local Mayan groups, the Pipil clearly spoke a version of Nahuatl, and worshipped Nahua deities.

---

or *atrio* adjacent to the church itself. Large numbers of indigenous followers mean that activities, like dramas, would necessarily have to occur outside of the church itself.

11   William R. Fowler, Jr. "Ethnohistoric Sources on the Pipil-Nicarao of Central America: A Critical Analysis." *Ethnohistory* 32(1):37-62. Both the Pipil of El Salvador and the Nicarao of Nicaragua are Nahuatl-speaking people from this migration. This article also lists most of the documentary evidence that indicates that the principle language of the Pipils was Nahuat.

In the records of the early Catholic church in El Salvador, San Esteban and the parish at Texistepeque are part of the one of the oldest centers for Roman Catholic mission in El Salvador. By 1546, the town of "Texistepeq" is listed among the towns falling under the ecclesiastical division of San Salvador.[12] In addition, early records indicate that some of the first clergy to come to El Salvador were trained in Guatemala (modern day El Salvador was part of the Spanish Empire administered by the authorities in Guatemala, who in turn were closely tied to Mexico) and trained in the indigenous languages of Mexico.[13] The Franciscans themselves were clearly in San Salvador by 1573 and possibly as early as 1553.[14] Therefore, there is every reason to believe that historically it would be possible for the practice of Nahua drama to be brought as an evangelization practice by these early priests and friars to Texistepeque.

There is no clear beginning date for the Talcigüines performance. Local people simply state that it has been performed for "at least one hundred years," or basically as long as anyone alive can remember. In 2015, the government of El Salvador actually gave it special status for being a part of the cultural patrimony of the nation. So, the performance is recognized as something unique to Texistepeque and quite old in terms of actual practice. Texistepeque is a small town in the Department of Santa Ana about 17 kilometers north of Santa Ana city on the main highway to Metapán. The town still has some cobblestone streets and a traditional town square surrounded by municipal buildings and the 18th century colonial style church of San Esteban. Since it lies a good deal inland from the coast, it has experienced little change over time, and remains primarily a rural agricultural town.

In terms of its connection to the Nahuatl language, the Talcigüines performance does not have any speaking parts, and is done entirely in pantomime; but the very name is Nahuatl in origin. It has been translated as "the demon possessed men," but its original meanings are probably much more obscure. As Burkhart mentions, "devils" in Nahuatl were called *tlatlacatecolo* (singular *tlacatecolotl*) by

---

12   Jesús Delgado Acevedo, *Historia de la Iglesia en El Salvador*, Biblioteca de Historia Salvadoreña, volumen 21, San Salvador: Dirección de Publicaciones e Impreses, (2013 reprint of a 2011 work), p. 136.

13   Ibid., p. 62. One record of a presbítero Martín Muñoz from 1583 indicates that he had served ten years in the parish of San Salvador in the work of evangelization and that he "knew the language of the Indians as if it was his own language."

14   Ibid., p. 74.

the Nahuatl speakers of Mexico.[15] But this term is not directly translatable to a Spanish understanding of demons or devils. For the Nahuatl speakers of Mexico, this term referred to human sorcerers who could transform themselves into owls. I do agree that the root word for the first part of the term "Talcigüines" is most likely *tlacat*, which can be translated as "devil" in the Spanish understanding of the term; however, I can find nothing to help translate the *güines* ending of the word. It is possible that the word has become corrupted over time, as no one in Texistepeque speaks Nahuatl today, but its origin is clearly not Spanish and is most likely rooted in Nahuatl.

THE TALCIGÜINES PERFORMANCE[16]

Early Monday morning on every Holy Week in Texistepeque, El Salvador, the performers who will play the Talcigüines begin to gather at the small colonial style church of San Esteban, which sits on the main square of the town. In a brief interview with one of the performers, it was made clear that this act is considered a very special honor and many of the performers are the sons and grandsons of men who have served this drama in the past. They must come early for confession before the Mass, where they take communion before the performance begins. Some of the performers seem to be in their 40's and others are as young a six or seven, but the majority are young men in their twenties.

---

15   Louise M. Burkhart, ed. *Aztecs on Stage: Religious Theater in Colonial Mexico,* 2011, Norman, OK: University of Oklahoma Press, p. 17.

16   All of the information and photographs in this section come from the author's field notes and personal observation when he attended the performance of the Talcigüines on Monday, May 30, 2015. Special thanks go to Moisés Antonio Godoy García, Kelly Jacqueline Godoy de Danielson, and Krissia Roxana Godoy Torres for taking photographs so the author could observe and interview participants.

Talcigüines Prepare their Outfits in the Church Courtyard

In the interview, I was also told that the performers are very respectful and that older people will not be whipped during the performance unless they give permission. If an older person is whipped without consent, it is usually because a friend of the person has encouraged the Talcigüin to whip them. For the most part, the Talcigüines will focus on young people in their teens or twenties (many of whom are personal acquaintances). During the Mass, the Talcigüines sit together in the front of the church along with the performer who plays Jesus. This performer has a great deal of respect in the community and has played the role for many years. He also appears to be training his son to take on this responsibility as well. Following the Mass, the Talcigüines put on their red cat-like masks and run out to the main town square from a side door in the church.

Roles Are Passed Down Through Families of Talcigüines

The outfits of the Talcigüines are short red tunics that extend to the knee and red hoods that cover the entire head. These hoods have cat-like ears and embroidered whiskers. From past images, I have sometimes seen what might be tails on the tunics, but in 2015 I did not observe any costumes like this. Each of the Talcigüines carry a short whip, and they often wear modern tennis shoes and t-shirts and shorts under the tunics because of the heat and the athleticism the performance requires. From about 9:00 AM to 12:00 noon, the Talcigüines will run throughout the town square and whip people at random. This often involves running, jumping, and sometimes acrobatics as they entertain the crowd. Given the high temperatures, they must exhibit a great deal of endurance to last three hours.

Mass is Held Before the Performance for the Costumed Performers

The people of the town and visitors gather in the main square of the town. There is a stage with musicians and vendors of various foods, drinks, candies, and toys for the children. There is also a special booth set up with t-shirts and handmade Talcigüines dolls, complete with red outfits and miniature whips. This is a festive atmosphere where people enjoy watching the whippings of the Talcigüines, even at the cost of getting one themselves. I have been told that local legend holds that for every lash received from a Talcigüin, God will forgive one sin from that person.

The Talcigüines primarily strike people on the legs with their whips. True to what I was told, older people are almost never struck, and young children might be touched lightly with the whip in a playful manner. The real targets seem to be young people, especially young men in their teens and twenties who are dressed in fashionable clothing and usually accompanied by friends or young ladies. Young women are also struck quite harshly, especially if dressed in shorts or with exposed legs. They were often targeted in a flirtatious way and seemed to enjoy the attention, even if they make a big commotion out of being struck. Many of the Talcigüines stop and take photos with visitors, and some older people encourage the performers to hit other friends or acquaintances of theirs. The audience played an active part in the performance as the targets of the Talcigüines, by watching the performance, and in some cases encouraging the Talcigüines to attack others.

The Talcigüines Torment People in the Public Square for Three Hours

About 12:00 noon, in the heat of the day, older women from the church began using hoses to water down the cobblestone road separating the church from the town square. They also use the hoses to wet the Talcigüines who were beginning to gather as well. As the Talcigüines began to act more lively and bring people into the street for whippings, the character of Jesus entered the scene from the left side of the church. He was dressed in a purple robe with a long black wig. In one hand he carried a small cross about ten inches high, and in the other hand he carried a small bell. Around his waist was tied a very thick rope that extended quite some distance behind him. Sometime earlier, he had emerged from the church and began to cleanse the sides and rear of the church. Now, at the front of the church, he begins to confront the Talcigüines one-on-one.

The Jesus figure confronts each Talcigüin in a crouching position, holding out the cross and ringing the bell, as if they were weapons. The Talcigüin runs back and forth seeking a way to approach and whip the Christ figure, but the Jesus character turns and continues facing the Talcigüin with the bell and cross. Finally, the Talcigüin falls onto the road, sometimes in very dramatic or acrobatic ways. Each falls down on a wet sheet placed in the road, laid out straight with their heads on their hands in an orderly row. Older women of the church straighten their tunics, give them bags of water and continue to hose them down because of the heat. When all of the Talcigüines have succumbed to the power of Christ, the Jesus character walks over the line of bodies pulling the thick rope over the entire line. At the end of the row the Talcigüines jump up and run into the church, and the performance is ended.

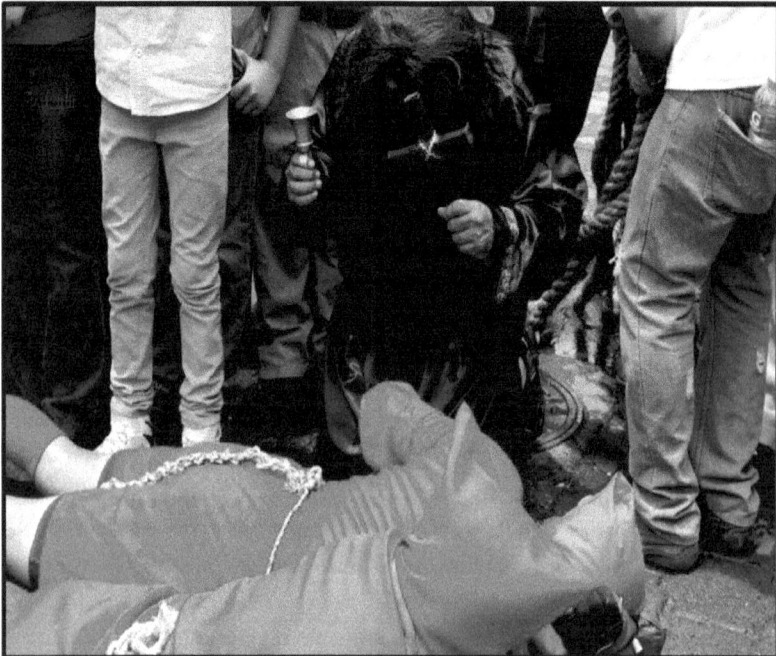

Jesus Confronts the Talcigüines at Noon in the Street in Front of the Church

Jesus Walks Over the Defeated Talcigüines Puling a Long Rope

SYMBOLISM AND SALVATION IN THE PUBLIC SQUARE

It is possible to read a great deal of symbolism into the Talcigüines performance from a loose reading of Nahua religious beliefs and cosmology, but some of that might be drawing conclusions that never really existed. It is also important to separate what might have been a traditional Pipil interpretation of the performance with its modern function in Texistepeque today.

There are several key things to keep in mind about El Salvador as we consider potential meaning and symbolism. First, Holy Week is typically the hottest time of the year and traditionally signals the beginning of the rainy season, so there may be traditional fertility symbols at work in this performance. Second, while the Pipil cosmology is not well known, the presence of several large clay statues of the god Xipe Totec[17] found in various archaeological sites may argue for a special focus on this deity.[18] Xipe Totec was an agricultural god associated with the fertility of spring and the planting of corn.[19] His name means "Our Lord, the Flayed One." Which comes from the Aztec practice of human sacrifice associated with the god. Priests or gladiators for Xipe Totec would wear the bloody flayed skins of sacrificial victims during his celebration, since he was believed to come to earth and wear human skin. The wearing of the flayed skin was related to the idea that corn must lose its husk before it can be planted to bring forth new life. In Mexico, mock gladiator combat would be held by warriors of Xipe Totec to sacrifice new victims.

It is curious that if the Talcigüines is a Nahua drama, it does not relate to any specific scriptural story. Jesus does heal demon-possessed men (Cf. Matthew 8:28-34, Mark 5:1-20, Mark 9:14-29, Luke 4:33-37, Luke 8:26-39) but nothing that seems to point to defeating a large group of such men in one biblical story. One would suspect that an allegorical play would have a consistent number of demons representing specific sins that plague human beings. Since there is not a clear biblical parallel, it does begin to look more like a contextualized drama that might have had strong original indigenous meaning. It is possible to see the Christ figure as a form of Xipe Totec sacrificing warriors in gladiatorial combat, whose red outfits may represent the flayed bodies needed for the fertility of the fields. On the other hand, the Christ figure may be defeating the warriors of Xipe Totec who are wearing the flayed skins of their sacrificial victims. This may also be a performance of Christ defeating the powers of evil represented by sorcerers who could transform

---

17   Paul E. Amaroli and Karen Olsen Bruhns. "Second Xipe Statue Found in El Salvador." *Mexicon* 26 (2): 24 (April 2004). This article notes that this is the 7th near-life-sized statue of Xipe Totec found in El Salvador, compared to only one of such size in Mexico.

18   It is only speculation on my part, but given the symbolism of Xipe Totec as a god who dressed in human skin to come among the people, it makes sense that early Nahua speakers would associate the incarnate Christ with Xipe Totec, and if this is the case, the choice of Christ as Savior of the World as the patron saint of El Salvador, might point to the close association of the Pipils with the worship of Xipe Totec. It is also interesting that in the local legends of El Salvador is a unique figure known as Cipitio, who is seen as a mischievous child with a large hat who eats ashes and whose feet face backwards. It is possible he also relates to some form of the god Xipe Totec, in part because he is not found in any other Latin American folklore outside of El Salvador.

19   Cf. with any major reference work. For a quick overview of Aztec and Mayan deities, see Clara Bezanilla, *Pocket Dictionary of Aztec and Mayan Gods and Goddesses*, J. Paul Getty Museum, 2010, p. 24.

themselves into jaguar type beings.[20] Either way, I think indigenous Nahua symbolism is clearly being used in this performance.

Whether for the original audience of recent Pipil converts, or the modern context, the Talcigüines drama does convey certain powerful images. For each audience, Christ is clearly the conqueror. No matter if the Talcigüines represent the need for fertility in agriculture or the forces of evil or temptation that attack all of us, Christ clearly prevails in this cosmic battle and brings salvation to the public square of Texistepeque. While the audience is partly passive observer, it is also active participant as well, as the people plagued by the forces of evil. Christ's actions replace the need for cosmic battles and bloody sacrifices.

In addition, the drama brings the community together, strengthens community identity, helps the local economy, and presents local visual religious symbols that everyone can understand at some level. Christ is not just the image of a saint confined to the sanctuary of the church building, especially using European imagery. The actor representing Christ becomes a type of living statue of a saint who walks out of the building and brings salvation to the people in the streets of the town itself. Not only that, but this Christ is clearly not European, but indigenous. While such a symbol may not be as powerful today as it was when the drama was created originally, it still has the ability to help us understand how such drama may have been a very effective evangelistic tool in early Spanish missions.

Conclusion

In conclusion, we can see many similarities between Burkart's description of Mexican Nahua dramas and the performance of the Talcigüines in Texistepeque, El Salvador. Like the Mexican historic dramas, the Talcigüines are performed on Holy Week, in this case on the Monday of Holy Week. While done in pantomime, the origin of the name is clearly Nahuatl in origin and tied to the religious symbols of human sorcerers who can change into animal forms, or to the Nahua deity Xipe Totec. The drama takes place in the public square, beginning in the church and moving out into the center of the town, which seems typical of many of the

20   While the Mexican term for such sorcerers implied they transformed into owls, the jaguar has a long history of religious symbolism within the Mayan world, and this may be reflected in the different geographical region of Nahua speaking people in El Salvador and their Mayan neighbors in Guatemala. Jaguars also were important in Aztec culture, with elite jaguar warriors being the men who performed the gladiatorial sacrifices for Xipe Totec. So the cat-like symbolism of the masks remains unclear.

Nahua dramas in Mexico, which took place outside of the immediate confines of the church in the larger community. In the same way, the larger community participates in the performance by watching and playing the role of the victims in the drama. Local people also play the major roles of both Jesus and the Talcigüines, with these roles often being hereditary within the family.

While its history cannot be directly traced back to the early years of Spanish mission, there is evidence of the early founding of San Esteban in Texistepeque and the early arrival of religious leaders trained in the languages and practices of Mexico at the same time as the Nahua dramas there. Given the similarity of culture between the Pipils and the Aztecs, it would be natural for similar methods of evangelization to be used.

While beyond the confines of this paper, I would argue that the ingenuity and creative use of drama by the early Spanish mission in the Americas, helps to argue for the need of more missiologists to re-examine and re-evaluate this early period of mission history. Ritual practices that have survived the test of time are probably not the best way to do this, but if they serve to remind us of how early mission evangelization practices brought salvation out of the church building and into the streets, perhaps they can also remind us of how much we can learn from mission history to impact contemporary evangelization in our current context.

Works Cited

Acevedo, Jesús Delgado
  2013 *Historia de la Iglesia en El Salvador, Biblioteca de Historia Salvadoreña*, volumen 21, San Salvador: Dirección de Publicaciones e Impreses, (Reprint of a 2011 work).

Amaroli, Paul E. and Karen Olsen Bruhns
  2004 "Second Xipe Statue Found in El Salvador." *Mexicon* 26 (2): 24 (April).

Bezanilla, Clara
  2010 *Pocket Dictionary of Aztec and Mayan Gods and Goddesses*, J. Paul Getty Museum.

Burkart, Louise M.
  1989 *The Slippery Earth: Nahua-Christian Moral Dialogue in Sixteenth-Century Mexico*. Tucson, AZ: The University of Arizona Press.

  1996 *Holy Wednesday: A Nahua Drama from Early Colonial Mexico*. Philadelphia, PA: University of Pennsylvania Press.

  2001 *Before Guadalupe: The Virgin Mary in Colonial Nahuatl Literature*. Institute for Mesoamerican Studies Monograph 13. Albany, NY: University at Albany.

Burkhart, Louise M., ed.
  2011 *Aztecs on Stage: Religious Theater in Colonial Mexico*. Norman, OK: University of Oklahoma Press.

Fowler, William R., Jr.
  1985 "Ethnohistoric Sources on the Pipil-Nicarao of Central America: A Critical Analysis." *Ethnohistory* 32(1): 37-62.

Mills, Kenneth and William Taylor, eds.
  1998 *Colonial Spanish America: A Documentary History*. Wilmington, DE: Scholarly Resources, Inc.

Schaller, John F.
    2010   "Evangelization as Performance: Making Music, Telling Stories," *The Americas* 66(3): 305-310 (Jan.).

The LDS Church and Public Engagement:

Polemics, Marginalization, Accomodation, and Transformation

Dr. Roland E. Bartholomew

DOI: 10.7252/Paper. 000076

The history of the public engagement of The Church of Jesus Christ of Latter-day Saints (also known as the "Mormons") is a study of their political, social, and theological shift from polemics, with the associated religious persecution and marginalization, to adjustments and accommodations that have rendered periods of dramatically favorable results. In two generations Mormonism went from being the "ultimate outcast"—its members being literally driven from the borders of the U.S. and persecuted abroad—to becoming the "embodiment of the mainstream" with members figuring prominently in government and business circles nationally and internationally; what one noted journalist has deemed "a breathtaking transformation."[1] I will argue that necessary accommodations made in Church orthodoxy and orthopraxy were not only behind the political, social, and theological "mainstream," but also consistently outlasted their "acceptability," as the rapidly changing world's values outpaced these changes in Mormonism.

1830-1889: MARGINALIZATION

The first known public engagement regarding Mormonism was when the young Joseph Smith related details regarding what has become known as his 1820 "First Vision" of the Father and the Son. He would later report that "my telling the story had excited a great deal of prejudice against me among professors of religion, and was the cause of great persecution."[2]

It may seem strange that Joseph Smith should be so criticized when, in the intense revivalistic atmosphere of the time, many people claimed to have received personal spiritual manifestations, including visions. But there was something else in Joseph Smith's story that the revivalist ministers did not like. The message that none of the local churches were right and that their creeds were an abomination in the sight of God did not fall on friendly ears among those who were preaching the revivals and contending for converts.[3]

Four years later Smith would claim a visit from an angel who delivered to him an ancient record engraven with reformed Egyptian hieroglyphs on metal

1   Verdoia, K. (2007) *The Mormons*, Part 2. Transcript of PBS Documentary. Available at: http://www.pbs.org/mormons/etc/script2.html (accessed 8 April 8, 2016).

2   Smith, J.S. (2013) *Joseph Smith History 1:22*. Salt Lake City: The Church of Jesus Christ of Latter-day Saints.

3   See Allen, J. and Leonard, G. (1992) *The Story of the Latter-day Saints*. Salt Lake City: Deseret Book, 35.

plates, produced by ancient American prophets. He also claimed angelic visitations from John the Baptist, Peter, James, John, and others. These assertions, along with the translation from the plates and subsequent publication of the Book of Mormon; and the establishment of a new church, all combined to intensify persecutions as the residents of Western New York saw friends and neighbors who not only believed Smith's claims, but also supported him financially and eventually joined his movement.

Subsequently Joseph Smith and his followers were forced to relocate to Ohio, near present day Cleveland. As his newly founded church continued to grow exponentially, so did the persecution. When his followers built a temple where ancient rituals were performed, and hundreds of his followers also reporting seeing visions, the persecution and suspicion among local residents intensified. Then Joseph's efforts to establish utopian communalism, along with a failed attempt at an anti-banking company, led to dissension from within. The lives of Joseph and his faithful followers were threatened, and they were driven out of Ohio by mobs consisting of disgruntled citizens and even some former members of the church.

While in Ohio, Joseph had conceptualized a millennial "City of Zion" to be founded in Independence, Jackson County, Missouri, which created panic among the residents of that region as Joseph's followers migrated there in large numbers, purchased over 24,000 acres, and boasted of the prophesied City of Zion and another temple. Understandably disturbed by what the locals saw as a threat to their political and economic interests, in 1834 they drove the Mormons out via "vigilante justice." Joseph's attempts at legal redress were denied in favor of rising public sentiment against the Mormons. After several failed attempts to establish permanent Mormon communities elsewhere in Missouri, church leaders were eventually incarcerated and the remaining Mormons were driven from the state by mobs and state militiamen, empowered by Governor Lilburn W. Boggs's infamous "extermination order," aimed at ridding the state of the "Mormon menace."

By the end of 1839 all Latter-day Saint prisoners had been released and the Mormons began gathering again, numbered in the thousands, in western Illinois and eastern Iowa. The Mormon city of Nauvoo was established under the protection of the government-sanctioned "Nauvoo Charter," and church members looked to a future of peaceful growth and prosperity. However, between the accusation that Joseph was complicit in the attempted assassination of former Governor

Boggs in Missouri—forcing Joseph into hiding—and the persecution from the formerly friendly residents of Hancock County (due to the high influx of new LDS converts) and the perceived evaporation of the locals' political influence and business interests, peaceful Mormon growth was short-lived. Tensions heightened as the Mormons rejected traditional political affiliations and Joseph Smith decided to run for United States president.

In an explosive political milieu, the Nauvoo Charter was revoked, the arms of the militia in Nauvoo were seized, Joseph Smith and his brother Hyrum were assassinated, and the Latter-day Saints were driven from Illinois and the confines of the United States. The reasons for these repeated violent rejections of Mormonism were deeply rooted: Mormonism was perceived in a predominantly rational protestant religious culture as being unorthodox, fanatical, and even demented—boasting faith healings, angelic visitations, speaking in tongues, and peculiar doctrines such as deification, plural marriage, and secretive temple rituals presumably borrowed from the Masons and altered to their own tastes. In addition, their "gathering to build a utopian communal Zion" was viewed as un-republican and in direct opposition to Jacksonian Manifest Destiny.

Led by Brigham Young, the majority of the Mormons migrated to the Great Basin between 1845 and 1847. They were followed by thousands of converts from the U.S., Canada and Europe. At last, they hoped they could live out their religion in peace and prosperity, isolated from the persecutions and influence of outsiders, while once again laboring to build up their utopian "Zion." But this hope quickly faded a few years later as the United States' westward expansion brought the Great Basin into US jurisdiction by the 1850 establishment of the Utah Territory, thus placing the Mormons under federal control, with anti-polygamy laws enforced upon them.[4]

1890-1949: Accommodation

Gradually, however, church leaders came to realize that for the church to survive, it would have to abandon controversial practices such as polygamy, utopian communalism, and theocracy. As a result of this accommodation, the end of the nineteenth century marked a major shift for the LDS Church, beginning a long process of enthusiastic assimilative movement into the American mainstream. In

4   See Reed, M.G. (2012) *Banishing the Cross: The Emergence of a Mormon Taboo.* Independence, MO: John Whitmer Books, 25.

1890 church president Wilford Woodruff received a revelation formally banning the practice of plural marriage among the Mormons, pledging allegiance to the US government and all its laws. This led to Utah acquiring statehood, being admitted into the Union on January 4, 1896.

As Mormons assimilated, opposition declined substantially, and by the second decade of the twentieth century the Mormon self-image had made an about-face. No longer playing the role of a rebellious sect standing apart from American norms and lifestyles, Mormons wanted to show the world they were even more American than other US citizens, and that they were just as Christian as Catholics and Protestants. This self-image has continued into the twenty-first century, but public perceptions have lagged substantially.[5]

For example, while the church was intentionally excluded from Chicago's 1893 World Parliament of Religions held in concert with the World's Columbian Exposition, it was provided a central location for agricultural and arts displays, which met with huge success. Additionally, The Mormon Tabernacle Choir finished second in the chorale competition, Mormon women were cast as critical allies of national female leaders, and Utah mining was extolled in superlatives. These temporal achievements helped downplay the church's unpopular theology, while the Mormons relished in their moment in the sun.[6]

However, in 1898 church leader B. H. Roberts, who had entered into plural marriage prior to the 1890 policy change and was still living with his plural wives, was elected to the US House of Representatives. By informal agreement after the church had terminated the practice of plural marriage, it was assumed—though not written into law—that in such cases men would not be punished so long as they entered into no new plural marriages. However, Protestant ministers in Utah accused him and the church of a breach of faith on the issue of polygamy, and after Roberts was elected they promoted a nationwide campaign against him, submitting to Washington a petition with seven million signatures. For six weeks after Elder Roberts arrived in Washington, a specially appointed committee held hearings and investigated the charges against him. In the end the House voted 268 to 50 not to seat him, and he was replaced by a non-Mormon monogamist.

---

5   See Reed, 25-26.
6   See Fluhman, S.J. (2012) *A Peculiar People: Anti-Mormonism and the Making of Religion in the Nineteenth Century.* Chapel Hill: UNCP, 131.

Four years later another church leader, Apostle Reed Smoot, was elected to the United States Senate. Even though Elder Smoot could categorically deny any involvement with plural marriage, he spent nearly five years defending the legality of his election in a Senate investigation. In the end, Senator Smoot retained his seat, despite the majority committee report which recommended his expulsion, because he was a leader in the LDS church.[7]

Despite that victory and the church's efforts to revamp its self-image, the church and its members continued to be presented to the public in popular magazines and novels in an unfavorable light, condemning polygamy or criticizing the leaders as autocrats and denouncing the church as un-American. To counteract the generally negative image still being promoted, The Church Bureau of Information and Church Literature on Temple Square opened on August 4, 1902, and the new information center became a significant force in building goodwill toward the Latter-day Saints. Eastern newspaper editors were among the thousands who went away impressed and so reported to their readers. In addition, the free guided tours of Temple Square helped promote the fame of the Tabernacle organ and the Salt Lake Mormon Tabernacle Choir. By the late 1920s annual visitors numbered 200,000.[8]

Despite these stepped-up efforts at public relations, the Church's image did not become fully positive during the 1920s.[9] Slowly, however, the tone of periodical literature seemed to be moving from hostility toward neutrality.[10] Then, during the 1930s the public image would become predominantly positive.

Perhaps the greatest boon to the church's public image, and what I believe was the turning point in public engagement, was the church's welfare plan that emerged during the dark days of the Great Depression. Church leaders created a security plan that would put their men back into the work force and make their members self-sufficient and independent of government welfare. During the first summer of its operation the LDS welfare program made impressive strides toward accomplishing these goals. Nearly fifteen-thousand needy Saints were transferred from government to church relief and more than one thousand were placed in jobs.

7   See Allen and Leonard, 444-447.

8   See Allen and Leonard, 451.

9   Shipps J. (2006) *Sojourner in the Promised Land: Forty Years among the Mormons.* Champaign: UIP, pp. 51-97.

10   See Allen and Leonard, 517-525.

Sufficient food, clothing, and fuel were collected via private donation to provide for practically all needy families through the coming winter. These accomplishments provided immediate and positive publicity for the church.[11] The growth of Mormon acceptance resulted from the new ways Americans saw Latter-day Saints as part of the national capitalist and imperial machine: Mormons could now be celebrated as industrious Americans. Selective forgetfulness, an appreciation of Mormons' temporal contributions, and an eye on future market possibilities made for a workable reconfiguration. In the eyes of many, a sober, efficient, and secularized Mormonism could emerge from its religious fanaticism and polygamous past and become at least partially respected for the ways it seemed to partake of the nation's modern corporate spirit.[12] For the first time, the total number of positive articles in American periodicals exceeded those with a negative viewpoint.[13]

1950 TO THE PRESENT: TRANSFORMATION

In 1950 a twelve-foot marble statue of Brigham Young was unveiled in the rotunda of the United States Capitol in Washington, D. C. Vice-President Alben W. Barkley honored Young as a "man of God" and an "advocate of justice and democracy," and one of Utah's "most eminent citizens, illustrious for his leadership as a colonizer." This was indeed a far cry from what national leaders had said about him and his followers a hundred years earlier.[14]

There were other, more general images of the Mormons being created in the 1950s. In national periodicals, there was a generally favorable public image, with the church being praised for its continuing activities in the welfare program. Also, successful Mormon businessmen and civic leaders were often favorably publicized with their church affiliation pointed out. Such was the case with J. Reuben Clark, Jr., a former undersecretary of state and American ambassador to Mexico, who was also known widely as a member of the church's First Presidency, and Elder Ezra Taft Benson of the Council of the Twelve Apostles who, in 1952, was appointed U.S. Secretary of Agriculture by the newly-elected Dwight D. Eisenhower. Other examples included the Mormon Tabernacle Choir, which received a Grammy award in 1959[15] and sang at Lyndon B. Johnson's inauguration in 1963.

11   See Allen and Leonard, 517-525.
12   See Fluhman, 144-46.
13   Allen and Leonard, 532.
14   See Allen and Leonard, 552.
15   See Allen and Leonard, 588-90.

During ensuing decades, church leaders felt a need to continuously engage publicly against such issues as the ERA, legalized abortion, gambling and homosexuality; and in favor of traditional marriage; These stances created new tensions with the mainstream. In addition, strains with evangelical Christianity, coupled with an emerging perception that the church was "controlling, powerful, wealthy, secretive" and "withholding information" about its history and practices caused a huge dip in public approval throughout the 1970s and 80s.[16] Nothing caused more strain, however, than the church's position regarding blacks and the priesthood. As civil rights emerged as a progressively pressing issue, the church's denial of its lay priesthood to black males became increasingly problematic and led to picketing, protests, and riots. Church president Spencer W. Kimball's 1978 revelation extending the priesthood to all worthy males, along with media-savvy church president Gordon B. Hinckley's continuously positive engagement with the media in the 1990s and early 2000s, alongside an equally open and persistent public relations campaign, all worked to placate negative stereotypes and helped return the church towards the mainstream. Prominent Mormons like the Osmonds, David Archuleta, Steve Young, Danny Ainge, Dale Murphy, Thurl Bailey and Gladys Knight also helped promote a more positive image. The highly successful 2002 Olympic Winter Games hosted in Salt Lake City provided yet another opportunity for positive public engagement.[17]

The Mormon Moment?

One noted scholar observed that no other new religious movement has navigated so adeptly both the rapids of religious growth and the still waters of mainstream respectability. Once almost universally hated, Mormons are now lionized as quintessentially American: "thrifty, wholesome, cooperative, industrious, purposeful, patriotic, law-abiding, God-fearing, well-organized and family oriented."[18]

However, in the end, Mormonism's efforts to become mainstream may yet have long-lasting, negative effects on its overall public engagement. So successful were Mormons at creating a public image that coincided with their self-

---

16   See Haws, J.B. (2103) *The Mormon Image in the American Mind: Fifty Years of Public Perception.* Oxford: OUP, 162 and 243.

17   See Haws, 171, 174.

18   Prothero, S. (2004) *American Jesus: how the Son of God Became a National Icon.* New York: McMillan, 187.

image, that by the time Mormon Mitt Romney sought the White House for a second time in 2012, he was labeled "the whitest white man to run for office in recent memory"[19]—a factor that undoubtedly contributed to him winning the Republican nomination but losing the election to the first black president in US History. What is more, decades of crafting the quintessential image of the "Family Church," which was mostly mainstream at its inception in the 1970s, has now left the church, once again, nearer the margins of an increasingly secular culture which appears to be abandoning traditional family values and definitions in favor of more "progressive" identity formations. In fact, according to *Newsweek*, "Despite the sudden proliferation of Mormons in the mainstream, Mormonism itself isn't any closer to gaining mainstream acceptance."[20]

CONCLUSION

Tensions relative to gender equality, sexual identity, and institutional distrust persist and continue to escalate into the twenty-first century. In the end, the history of the LDS church's public engagement is the story of initial polemics, resulting in marginalization, followed by accommodations and astounding transformations, which, interestingly and significantly, could result in a return to polemics and marginalization, if church orthodoxy and orthopraxy continue immutable.

---

19   See Reeve, W.P. (2015) *Religion of a Different Color: Race and the Mormon Struggle for Whiteness.* Oxford: UOP.

20   Kern, W. (2011) The Mormon Moment. *Newsweek*, June 5, 2011.

Public Theology or Private Bewitchment?

East African Christian Diaspora Views on the Opportunities and Dangers of Social Media

Grant Miller and Reuben Lang'at

DOI: 10.7252/Paper. 000077

In her popular song and video "Facebook," Rose Muhando, Tanzania's most famous Christian revival singer, warns of the potential dangers of social media as a threat to Christian faith and community. The video comically and tragically depicts pastors and lay Christians alike distracted by phones and computers as they reject and ignore spouses, friends and loved ones who desperately vie for their attention. For the past eighty years the East African Revival has promoted and nurtured Christian community and accountability in Tanzania. Now, many Tanzanian Christians see social media as a tool with the potential to destroy families and communities. In this song, Muhando laments the overuse of Facebook, Twitter and Whatsapp Messenger as she repeatedly sings the question, "*Hivi nani aliyewaloga?*" ("Who bewitched you?") The answer is emphatic and clear: "*Ni utandawazi!*" (It was globalization!) Muhando's warning illustrates how many Christians in Tanzania and throughout East Africa emphasize that faith must be lived out in community in ways that simultaneously critique and shape public life.

In this age of intensified globalization, increasing numbers of Tanzanians and Kenyans are also using the Internet and social media to explore and seek academic and professional opportunities outside of East Africa, often in the United States. Many join transnational, diaspora communities that use social media as a lifeline to stay connected with family and friends scattered across the globe. For those living transnational lives, social media provides a borderless and virtually instant mode of communication. While Christians from East Africa are well aware of the potential dangers of the misuse of social media, many in diaspora contexts have a more positive view of social media as they appreciate its power to help them maintain a sense of belonging in transnational communities scattered across continents. Social media is also a powerful tool that allows Kenyans and Tanzanians to share their faith in ways that engage with and critique public life both at home and in diaspora.

OUR PERSONAL INTERESTS AND ORIGINS OF THE STUDY

When I (Reuben) was a young boy, growing up in Kenya, our means of communication were those that had been passed down from previous generations. The main method of communication was in the oral form. If a major event like a death, wedding or circumcision had happened or was planning to happen in a village, the family would tell a messenger who would travel to inform other family members in other villages. Information would generally spread through word of mouth except during some instances when the elders would use smoke signals to communicate certain information.

Times have changed since then and culture has tremendously evolved. When my family and I moved from Kenya to United States in 2004, the use of social media was not as prevalent as it currently is especially in Kenya, but rapid change has taken place within the past twelve years. These changes in the use of technology have changed not only how people communicate and socialize; it has affected other areas of society such as the banking system, the spread of the Gospel and other areas. Virtually all Kenyans, ranging from the elite in the city to those in the villages who do not speak English, own a cell phone and use it for branchless banking with M-Pesa, a mobile money transfer service that is extremely popular in East Africa. Millennials now easily plan political protests through the use of Facebook, Instagram and Twitter. Analog television sets in Kenya have been upgraded and almost everyone has gone to digital systems. Gospel artists, preachers and evangelists can now easily spread the gospel through different media platforms.

After serving full-time in partnership with the Morogoro Diocese of the Evangelical Lutheran Church in Tanzania from 2000 to 2008, I (Grant) transitioned into a volunteer role. I have returned to Morogoro for brief visits every year since. In 2009, on a flight from London to Dar es Salaam (Tanzania's global city), I was seated next to a Tanzanian man who shared that he was returning to Tanzania for the first time since he had emigrated in 1995. He had been living near two older siblings outside of London. When I asked him if he and his siblings were able to connect with other Tanzanians living in the United Kingdom, he looked at me almost dumbfounded and said, "Sure." When I proceeded to ask him exactly how they were able to connect, assuming he would mention an African diaspora congregation, he answered, "There is a website." (Miller 2016) Five years later, in 2014, I began interviewing Tanzanians living in the United States. When I asked the very first Tanzanian I spoke with how he stayed connected with family and friends scattered across multiple continents, he proudly showed me WhatsApp Messenger (an app specifically and harshly criticized in Muhando's song) on his phone and spoke of how essential this free app and service was for those living in diaspora.

This informal study focuses on how Kenyan and Tanzanian Christians in diaspora contexts view and use social media today. This paper will explore how these members of the East African Christian diaspora in America view social media as a tool not just for maintaining social capital, but also for maintaining spiritual capital they have experienced and developed in ministries flowing out of the East African Revival. In the ministries of the ongoing East African Revival, social capital and spiritual capital of the Christian community are intertwined and inseparable. Private faith and public faith are also inseparable as religion is not relegated or limited to private spheres in Kenya and Tanzania. In diaspora, Christians from East Africa use social media to help them maintain spiritual capital even as they remain aware of its potential to "bewitch" and "brainwash" users. We will explore how social media helps to connect isolated individuals and groups of the East African Christian diaspora by providing them with forums for prayer, accountability and community-building as well as for the expression and sharing of grassroots public theologies and public faith.

A Gap in African Christian Diaspora Literature

Afe Adogame (2011, 2013) and J. Kwa Bena Asamoah-Gyadu (2013, 2015) have both written invaluable and extensive accounts of West African Pentecostalism. Adogame (2011, 2013) has described the use of social media in the development of global, transnational ministries both in West Africa and in diaspora. Few, however, have conducted such in-depth studies of the smaller East African Christian diaspora, influenced by the unique legacy of the East African Revival, an ongoing evangelical awakening. As studies on the African Christian diaspora become increasingly common, there is a need for more extensive studies of the smaller East African diaspora.

From 2008-2009, while 201,000 Nigerians and 110,000 Ghanaians were admitted to the United States, only 68,000 Kenyans and merely 10,000 Tanzanians were admitted during the same period (Capps, McCabe, Fix 2011: 4). As Nigerians, Ghanaians and others from West Africa living in the United States greatly outnumber Kenyans, Tanzanians and others from East Africa, it is not surprising that the majority of studies on African diaspora Christianity in the United States focus on West African immigrant churches. These studies include *Beyond Christendom: Globalization, African Migration, and the Transformation of the West* (Hanciles 2008); *Word Made Global: Stories of African Christianity in New York City* (Gornik 2011); *The African Christian Diaspora: New Currents and Emerging Trends in World Christianity*

(Adogame 2013); *Scattered Africans Keep Coming: A Case Study of Diaspora Missiology on Ghanaian Diaspora and Congregations* (Wan and Edu-Bekoe 2013). We hope this small study will highlight an important gap in literature on the African Christian diaspora that has often concentrated heavily on the larger West African Christian diaspora. Kenyans and Tanzanians from East Africa have their own unique diaspora stories, theologies, ministries and contributions that have yet to be shared and heard on a large scale.

Like Adogame (2013, 161) in his research on the West African Christian diaspora, this paper will use transnational theory to explore practices of "religious transnationalism from below" at the micro- and meso- levels of community as we shift the focus to the East African Christian diaspora and the unique legacy of the East African Revival. We will specifically describe how Kenyan and Tanzanian individuals, families, and congregations in America use social media both privately and publicly as they develop and share both private and public faith living transnational lives in an increasingly interconnected world.

THE KENYAN AND TANZANIAN CHRISTIAN DIASPORAS

Kenyans and Tanzanians, like many Africans in diaspora, often leave East Africa in search of higher education. Social media allows them to communicate with friends and family who have already successfully studied in diaspora. According to a research study conducted by the Migration Policy Institute, "the number of African immigrants in the United States has grown 40-fold between 1960 and 2007, from 35,355 to 1.4 million…compared to other immigrants, the African born tend to be highly educated and speak English well" (Terrazas 2009, 1). Research further indicates that two of every ten African-born adults in the United States has earned at least a bachelor's degree or higher. Not only do many hold an academic degree, most of them are employed in the civilian labor force in jobs including management, business, finance, physician, nurse, administrative support and manufacturing, just to name a few (Terrazas 2009, 1). For example, thirty percent of Kenyans in the United States over the age of 25 hold a bachelor's degree (compared to twenty percent in the American population overall) while sixteen percent hold a master's degree, PhD or advanced professional degree (compared to only eleven percent of the American population) (Migration Policy Institute 2015: 6).

Religion still plays a huge role in the lives of most Africans, including the highly educated. Therefore, even though some might not be sure of their identity in diaspora, most will refer back to their spiritual roots and hold that as their identity. According to Walters and Auton-Cuff (2009: 764), "religion potentially offers ideologies, relationships, and spirituality necessary for identity formation, helping to trigger considerations of identity issues as well as suggesting resolutions for identity concerns. It is not rare to see churches started by Africans in different communities in the States. Africans can find identity amidst these churches because it is where they find a sense of belonging in the first place; it is where they can find support as they transition because almost everyone in the church is going through the phase together. Russell and Bartchy (2014: 4) refer to this phase as liminality. Individuals in liminality "do not have structural status and roles… they often exhibit properties of homogeneity, equality, anonymity, and absence of property." Most of the Kenyans living in diaspora can be described as living in what Stephane Dufoix calls "enclaved mode" meaning a local community in a host state or country, that "operates locally and helps its participants to get to know and stay in touch with one another" (Dufoix 2008: 63). Members share the same identity or place of origin and while they live in a host country they keep in touch through social media and other means. The atopic mode "refers to a way of being in the world between states that is built around a common origin, ethnicity, or religion that does not reduce one to being a subject of a host country" (Dufoix 2008: 63). This also appropriately describes diaspora life for many Kenyans who live in groups in different states in the US, but are connected to other groups in other states, who all share the same country of origin, culture, and faith. For example, the Kenyan Christian Fellowship in America, has different chapters in different states, but gathers for an annual conference each year.

The Tanzanian diaspora in the United States is even smaller than the Kenyan diaspora. As a small minority in the larger African meta-diaspora, Tanzanians can easily become quite isolated from other Tanzanians geographically. As a result, Tanzanians often worship in Kenyan and East African diaspora congregations. Even in small numbers, however, Tanzanians strive to worship, pray and meet together as Tanzanians united by the common, national language of Swahili as often as possible. They often travel great distances to celebrate and mourn together at graduations, weddings and funerals. Tanzanians organize their own hometown associations as well as regional and national conferences. They highly value inclusiveness, inter-ethnic harmony and inter-faith cooperation in these communities that demonstrate a strong desire to express public faith.

As Kenyan and Tanzanian Christians have all been influenced by the legacy of the East African Revival, they strive to maintain core elements of their culture and religious faith and spirituality as they live in diaspora. In Kenya and Tanzania, all faith is a public faith that engages with and critiques public life. Many people in the world today are "increasingly unwilling to keep their convictions and practices limited to the private sphere of family or religious community" (Volf 2011: ix). Diaspora life can be a struggle for many Kenyans and Tanzanians as they live in an American culture that often discourages people from sharing faith in public spheres and often values individual freedom above both faith and community.

A Brief History of the East African Revival and its Legacy

Kenyans and Tanzanians living today were born and raised during a time of remarkable church growth throughout their entire region and continent. In 1900, there were only 10 million Christians in Africa. Only a century later, in 2000, there were 400 million (Shaw 2010: 11). This number continues to grow as roughly half of the continent professes faith in Christ-making Africa arguably the world's most Christian continent today. As Africa became a Christian continent, Christianity in East Africa spread very rapidly in a very short time. The East African Revival became one of the many global awakenings "at the heart of the global resurgence of Christianity" (Shaw 2010: 12). In East Africa the numerical growth of Christianity between 1914 and 1944 was "phenomenal" (Oliver 1952: 234). By 1938, when the East African Revival entered Tanzania, about ten percent of the population of Tanganyika (the name for Tanzania from 1922 until 1964) and eight percent of the population of Kenya was already Christian. As revival flourished, indigenous pastors, evangelists and lay leaders, spread the gospel quickly with great passion. Overall, the percentage of Christians in East Africa rose rapidly from 15.9 percent in 1910 to 64.7 percent in 2010 (Johnson and Ross 2009).

Kevin Ward (1991, Wild-wood and Ward 2010, 2013) has written extensive accounts of the history of the East African Revival, especially its early and rapid spread throughout Uganda. As the East African Revival flowed from Uganda into Tanzania in 1938, it emphasized holiness and accountability in community. In the 1970s, this emphasis on holiness and accountability combined with a sudden, new emphasis on the power of the Holy Spirit to heal sicknesses and deliver demons. Many experienced healing and deliverance at this time and shared testimonies reminiscent of the events in the book of Acts. These powerful testimonies drew even more to the Christian faith and the church continued to grow rapidly throughout East Africa. The 1990s, the end of the Cold War and the age of the Internet and intensified globalization ushered in the age of global charismatic/Pentecostal churches that shared this emphasis on the power of the Holy Spirit to heal and deliver. Kalu (2011: 107) noted, "Perhaps, Pentecostalism has picked up the core elements of Evangelicalism and imbued them with new life." Many Tanzanian Christians in diaspora stress this combination and balance of the "sound" biblical teaching of global evangelicalism with the passion and freedom of global Pentecostalism (Miller 2016). Many indicated that just as evangelicalism that ignores the power of the Holy Spirit is lifeless, Pentecostalism that ignores sound biblical teaching is dangerous. Many Tanzanian Christians see that Evangelicalism and Pentecostalism are both necessary as each emphasis compliments and balances the other.

Another lasting legacy of this ongoing evangelical awakening in East Africa is the emphasis on Christian community and unity. As traditional life in Africa was always communal, Christians in Africa are quick to notice and embrace the strong emphasis on community and communal life described throughout the Bible. Just as they do back in Tanzania, Tanzanians in diaspora place a high value on gathering to celebrate and mourn together. Weddings and funerals are extremely important community events in diaspora just as they are back home. Tanzanians emphasized, "every celebration is a community celebration and every tragedy is a community tragedy" (Miller 2016). Tanzanian pastor Elieshi Mungure (2011: 442), who ministered to the East African diaspora in the United States describes the essence of what she calls "African relational theology" stating, "Life is recognized as life in community. To be truly human is to be true to ones own community."

For many Christians from Africa, these communities include communities of prayer and worship. One young woman from Tanzania, who frequently worships in a Kenyan congregation in diaspora, explained, "I can't leave church on Sunday until I have taken time to speak to everyone and make sure everyone is doing well." While stressing the importance of these face-to-face interactions, she also praised social media as a means of staying connected with family and friends scattered in diaspora and back home in East Africa.

THE USE OF SOCIAL MEDIA BY THE KENYAN AND TANZANIAN DIASPORAS: NO ONE REJOICES OR MOURNS ALONE

In diaspora, social media becomes an essential tool for Christians from East Africa who value the biblical call to rejoice and mourn together. Acknowledging weddings and funerals and major life events even when isolated and distant physically helps them maintain social capital and a sense of belonging of community. Even when they are unable to attend these important events in person, Christians from East Africa can use social media to let family and friends know that they are still thinking of them and still value being a member of distant communities. Even in diaspora, Christians from East Africa want to ensure that no one rejoices or mourns alone. Diaspora pastors often use social media to reach out to young members of their congregations who can become isolated and lost in diaspora. Pastors use social media to frequently remind members that even when they quit attending church, people are still praying for them and ready to welcome them any time they choose to return. Even when some choose to isolate themselves in diaspora, communication through social media can remind them that they are never forgotten or alone.

Kenyan and Tanzanian diaspora communities of faith provide social, cultural, and spiritual capital far from home. Adogame (2013: 106) explains, "Generally, religious capital is associated with the investment an individual makes in his/her religious faith and organization." He adds, "Spiritual capital energizes religious capital by providing a theological identity and worshiping tradition, but also a value system, a moral vision and a basis for faith…embedded locally within religious and faith-based groups, but…also expressed in the lives of individuals" (Adogame 2013: 106). Social, cultural, religious, and spiritual capital should be understood as "interconnected" and "dovetailing…in practical terms" (Adogame 2013: 106). Kenyan and Tanzanian diaspora communities demonstrate this interconnectedness and "dovetailing."

For example, Kenyans in Kentucky have come together to form an annual gathering. The gathering is usually planned by a small group of committee members. The aim of the gathering is simply to fellowship, provide an avenue for networking, and celebrate shared Kenyan heritage. They usually invite a keynote speaker who talks about an issue affecting them. Some of the issues that have been addressed by this community include "how to navigate through immigration issues, how to raise children in America who might be going through marginality, and how to live in diaspora. Many of these immigrants are interested in investing in Kenya while they are living in the States. This shows that it is becoming easier and easier to be transnational, especially because we are at the peak of globalization" (Lang'at 2015: 7). For example, last year's (2015) topic was "Heritage and Education as Foundations for Success and a New Identity." This year, the topic will be "Investment Opportunities for Kenyans living in Diaspora." They utilize the resources available by requesting Kenyans in the community who have experience in particular topics to be speakers. Kenyans who attend range from well-educated professors, lawyers, doctors, students, and those who recently arrived from Kenya.

Many members of Kenyan and Tanzanian diaspora communities also share a commitment to rejoice, mourn, and worship together. For example, Kenyans in a small American city quickly mobilized to help a Kenyan woman who suddenly and tragically lost her husband while living in diaspora. They provided this widow with spiritual as well as social and financial support. Tanzanian communities frequently do the same as they mobilize quickly to celebrate with those who celebrate and mourn with those who mourn. Tanzanians in diaspora support those who have lost family members back home and frequently help them with funeral and travel expenses. A Tanzanian pastor spoke of cancelling important church events in order to help his congregation support and mourn together with a young woman in their community after she suffered a devastating miscarriage in diaspora far from her traditional support network back home.

While social/cultural capital is extremely important in diaspora communities, for many raised in the East African Revival, the spiritual capital through constant prayer and accountability provided by these communities is as important, if not more important, than social/cultural capital (Miller 2016: 128). For many in the East African Christian diaspora, social capital, and spiritual capital are indeed interlocked, intertwined and inseparable. A Kenyan professor explained how fellowship without prayer is empty just as prayer without true fellowship is lacking.

Social media helps many Kenyans and Tanzanians in diaspora mobilize to meet and support one another in times of need. Many Africans in diaspora use the Internet as a "complimentary vehicle" rather than a replacement for interpersonal bonds and social networks (Adogame 2011: 235). It can also help many who are truly isolated maintain a sense of fellowship while providing prayer support at a distance. In communal diaspora communities, someone might put a prayer request on social media, but still prefer meeting with a person face-to-face to share more and pray together. In fact, some find more courage to post prayer requests on social media. These posts can prompt friends to call them, or meet with them in person if possible, to speak and pray in greater detail.

The transnational practice of African Christian phone prayer groups has emerged as a vital and unique diaspora phenomenon and innovation (Miller 2016). Almost every one of the Tanzanians I interviewed in diaspora described how they join prayer groups by phone almost daily, with the option of joining two to three times a day. While descriptions varied slightly, one pastor gave a typical example explaining how through a ministry of their congregation, approximately twenty-five people will join together by phone for about thirty minutes, three times a day at 6:00 AM, 1:00 PM and 7:30 PM, seven days a week to hear scripture, a short sermon and then share prayer requests and prayer. Another Tanzanian pastor on the East Coast of the United States explained that they start every day with a phone prayer line that regularly draws over forty participants from as many as eighteen different states.

Through the ministries of these phone prayer lines, often organized and connected through social media, Tanzanians in diaspora, who may not be as able to meet in person as they are back in Tanzania, regularly pray for and receive healing and breakthroughs just as they do at worship services. These phone prayer lines provide a way for Tanzanians to experience and share in some way the spiritual capital and accountability provided by the Christian communities they value so highly, even at a distance, when logistics in diaspora make meeting in person difficult (Miller 2016).

I (Grant) had never heard of this practice during my seventeen years of ministry experience in Tanzania. When I asked one man if he had ever participated in these phone prayer lines back home, he said that he too had only heard of this practice since arriving in diaspora. He said that back home it is easier to meet for prayer in person and that even though he was a very successful and busy civil servant in Dar es Salaam, he still met with friends to pray during lunch almost every day. Others confirmed that these phone prayer lines have emerged out of necessity as a unique African Christian diaspora practice and phenomenon.

Pastors often lead these groups and times of prayer, but also delegate responsibilities to laity. Many Tanzanians in diaspora participate in several different phone prayer lines. One man, who is quite isolated from other Tanzanians in diaspora, explained how his sister told him about a great phone prayer line led by a Kenyan woman living in a completely different region of the United States far from where he lives. Another man explained how there are so many different prayer lines here now that many have started prayer phones lines just for specific needs. For example, he said many women have started their own prayer lines just for women. Many of the Tanzanians I spoke with also mentioned using these phone prayer lines to share prayer requests as they pray for American neighbors, co-workers, and friends.

While almost every Tanzanian I interviewed reported being blessed by these phone prayer lines in the United States, a few also noted drawbacks. At least two people I interviewed voiced concern that some can be tempted to use these phone prayer lines in the place of personal prayer and devotion. They worried that people could rely on these phone prayer lines alone as a substitute for private prayer. Another explained it is difficult for leaders to know everyone who joins, so that privacy and confidentiality become an issue. Political prayers can also cause tensions, especially during election years. In the end, however, people spoke in overwhelmingly positive terms regarding these prayer phones lines. When I specifically asked about the efficacy of these phone prayer lines, one Tanzanian pastor stressed emphatically, "People receive healing through these prayers" (Miller 2016: 140).

Kenyans also use social media to organize and facilitate phone prayer lines regularly, often weekly. A number of prayer lines have been formed to bring Kenyans and their friends together in prayer. Those who are here in the USA and those in Kenya and other African countries are able to connect through WhatsApp or Skype and pray together. Tanzanians often find and join these Kenyan-led phone prayer groups just as they often join Kenyan congregations. Tanzanians, who are even more scattered and isolated in diaspora, may be even more reliant on prayer by phone than Kenyans, who can more easily form their own diaspora congregations.

In spite of extensive use of social media and phones in prayer groups by Tanzanian and Kenyan Christians in diaspora, I (Grant) have so far found only one specific reference to these phone prayer lines in the literature on African diaspora Christianity. Mark Gornik (2011: 133) describes how a woman from Ghana who works the night shift, "returns home and sleeps briefly, waking up at 8:00 a.m. for morning prayers." He explains, "But instead of travelling to the church, she dials a telephone number that switches her into a prayer meeting with between four and nine fellow members. Over the telephone, they pray for everyday needs." Gornik's description reflects both the willingness to sacrifice sleep for God and the appreciation for phone prayer lines that I heard from the Tanzanians I interviewed who often face new cultural and logistical obstacles in diaspora, preventing them from meeting with fellow Christians in person daily.

"FACEBOOK CHURCH" AND INTERACTIVE COMMUNICATIONS

Interconnectedness has been enhanced in this age of globalization. People and other things can be localized, but the Internet cannot. The Internet keeps people connected regardless of where they are in this global world. Interpersonal relationships can be kept going regardless of where the people are (Eriksen 2015: 103). This interconnectedness has helped those who live in diaspora stay connected with the family, relatives, and friends in their home countries. There are a number of Kenyans who have "closed" Facebook groups so as to help them keep the discussions going in the areas of their interests. I am sure this is not limited only to Kenyans. A number of Kenyan artists have used social media (YouTube) to share their talents and even sell their music. This has become a source of encouragement to many who would not have had a privilege of sharing their needs with those who are separated by miles from their friends or family members.

I recently talked to a pastor who migrated to the US a number of years ago, but has kept reaching out to his church members back home through Facebook and he said, "At times I preach through Skype on Sundays." The distant has been greatly reduced by the Internet. A World Gospel Mission missionary and his wife, who have served in Kenya for many years, took a challenge a few years back and started a "Facebook Church" in which they reach out to many people within Kenya and outside. They have been able to write and post Christian materials for their friends and offer counseling helps using social media. They told me they were very excited about the opportunity to reach out to so many regardless of where they live in this global world.

A Kenyan woman recently saw a need at one of the hospitals in Kenya and shared it on her Facebook page. Within a few days, an American family in another state shared it and took the need to her Sunday school. Within just a few weeks, they were able to raise over $1,000 to help meet the need. Social media used well can be of great help in sharing the needs that we have with people that we don't even know, and God can lead them to provide. There are a number of bishops who live in diaspora, but through the Internet, they are able to connect and worship and even do evangelism as well as pastoral care online with some of their followers who can access social media. Internet is borderless and a virtually instant mode of communication for those who live distant from each other.

While Tanzanians in diaspora generally view social media as a good way to stay connected to communities both here and back home, Tanzanians living in Tanzania still have a more jaded view of social media reflected in Muhando's very popular song. She describes globalization as bewitching Christians and vividly describes how Facebook and the WhatsApp Messenger lead to the ruin of ministries and marriages. She explains Facebook, Twitter and WhatsApp Messenger have become "*mungu wa kanisa la leo* (the god of today's church)" and "*kichaa kamili kwa kizazi cha leo* (complete insanity for today's generation)." Muhando's video vividly portrays pastors checking Facebook and emails in the pulpit while members of the congregation raise one hand in praise even as they use the other hand to check messages on their mobile phones. Similarly, Adogame (2013: 122) describes a notice at a Nigerian Redeemed Christian Church of God church stating, "Please switch off your mobile phones. The only urgent call expected here is the voice of God." While these issues are not unique to Tanzania or even Africa, they are very real. Recently, Tanzanian pastors in Tanzania have confirmed that these concerns expressed by Muhando are genuine.

Tanzanians living in diaspora in the United States do not seem to share this level of concern regarding social media found in home contexts. On the contrary, many described social media as an absolutely essential tool to demonstrate belonging and concern as members of scattered communities in diaspora. Kenyans and Tanzanians in diaspora share positive views of social media in diaspora contexts. At the same time, they are all very aware of its potential dangers and abuses. Some lamented time they simply wasted time on Facebook, while others noted Facebook promoted the formation and acceptance of more superficial and distant relationships. Others mentioned the dangers of addiction to pornography and the temptation to form unhealthy relationships that can be hidden and sustained through the use of social media (portrayed in Muhando's video).

AMERICAN CONCERN ABOUT SOCIAL MEDIA

Concern regarding the overuse and abuse of social media is a global issue that is not unique to Africa. Americans of all generations are often equally overwhelmed and confused with how to adapt and respond to social media as a rapidly growing part of global life today. Mark Bauerlein, author of *The Dumbest Generation*, vividly points out that in April of 2003 Americans spent zero minutes on Facebook, while just six years later, in April of 2009 Americans logged in 13,872,640,000 minutes (Bauerlein 2011: x). The world soon followed.

Facebook boasts it now has 1.5 billon users, which is roughly half of the world's 3.17 billion Internet users (Buchanan 2015). WhatsApp Messenger is used by 1 billion people worldwide and claims "nearly one in seven people on Earth… now use WhatsApp each month to stay in touch with their loved ones, their friends, their family" as they send and receive text, photos and video "without paying steep fees to local wireless carriers" (Metz 2016).

Through social media, people of all ages around the globe create "modern self portraits" that are highly "interactive" as they demand our response (Rosen 2011: 173). This instant and constant ability to seek and receive attention has created an incessant flood of both positive and negative messages and images. In 1979, long before social media, Dr. Aaron Stern (1979) warned of enabling the "Narcissistic American." No one seems to have listened. Thirty years later, Twenge and Campbell (2009) wrote about the "The Narcissim Epidemic" fueled by social media. Now we have a "digital divide" (Bauerlein 2011) and "digital vertigo" (Keen 2012) as social media is "dividing, diminishing and disorienting us." Finally, we were all shocked to hear that "selfie deaths" outnumbered shark attack deaths in 2015 (Breslin 2015).

The warnings have been there all a long, and long before the birth of the Internet. As noted, thirty years ago, Stern (1979: 140) stated that as American media is "the most powerful and pervasive in the world," and one that "sympathetically vibrates with…innate narcissistic forces," we should not be surprised to find that America has "come to be regarded as the most narcissistic nation of all." Stern's (1979: 145) proposal was simple; "If we demand expression of more loving values, we can control the growing narcissistic infestation spread by the media. If we don't make that demand, the narcissistic infestation will not only continue, it will grow and overcome us all." Social media has certainly played a major role in the "growing narcissistic infestation" spreading through global culture and society.

Many Americans find social media to be "an architecture of human isolation" rather than of the community it projects so that we are "schizophrenic… simultaneously detached from the world and yet jointly ubiquitous" online (Keen 2012: 14). Relating the terror and fears of many parents today, a father who just allowed his teenage daughter to join Facebook for the first time noted he felt as if he had "passed her a pipe of crystal meth" (Keen 2012: 173). The power and freedom to present ourselves as whoever we want to be, instantly and everywhere at once on social media does indeed become intoxicating to many, and many find themselves addicted.

Social media can negatively affect families, relationships, and communities quickly. Twenty percent of new divorce cases "reference inappropriate sexual conversations on Facebook as a factor in the marriage breakup" (Keen 2012: 68). Muhando's video clearly shows this reality as well. Life online can also harm true personal relationships and community as social media promotes and facilitates fleeting, superficial, low-risk relationships in cyberspace.

While social media may encourage and enable "shallowness and narcissism" it can also promote and facilitate healthy connections and collaboration across borders instantaneously (Twenge and Campbell 2009: 121-122). East African Christians in diaspora have realized and capitalized on the positives even as they are aware of the dangers. Americans see these positives as well and some are even learning from the rest of the world how to use social media in positive and constructive ways. Palfrey and Gasser (2011: 190-191) note how the large diaspora community of Kenyans "use the internet as a primary means of communication… in highly sophisticated ways geared toward having a political impact."

Around the globe, young people are beginning to influence the course of important events, demonstrating that "when a lot of people care passionately about something the Internet can become a powerful tool of organization, recruitment, and participation in the telling of the narratives of our society" (Palfrey and Gasser 2011: 203). The East African Christian diaspora has realized this but also understand that political activism, like community and fellowship, is always lacking without the power of prayer and the foundation of biblical truth. Kenyans and

Tanzanians in diaspora share not only their own narratives but also their belief that their stories, and all of our stories, must be understood as part of God's larger story. The prayers and testimonies that Kenyans and Tanzanians share on social media are a form of public faith and theology visible to all as they quickly become "friends" with people all over the globe.

Many believe that media should be understood as the "connective tissue of society" today (Shirky 2015: 329). Social media truly connects people as never before, but we are left with questions regarding what kind of connections we want. Do we want our connections and communities to be living tissue that is healthy and growing organically or unhealthy, fleeting, and artificial. Communities of the East African Christian diaspora are grappling with these issues. They can help Americans and the larger body of Christ as they seek true spiritual capital that is never isolated from social and cultural capital in person or online.

In 1993, Robin Dunbar of Oxford University found that a group of 150 individuals seems to be the "optimal social circle for which we are wired as a species." Furthermore, "Dunbar's number" as we now call this "optimal number of complex relationships that our brains can effectively manage" has remained constant throughout human history (Keen 2012: 175). From "neo-lithic villages" to "Roman legions," humans have only ever been capable of managing approximately 150, personal, face-to-face relationships. Even in our new global village, our human brains simply cannot keep up with the technology of social networks (The Economist 2016: 74). In today's increasingly interconnected world, our small, personal social networks as well as our large, impersonal social networks are all becoming increasingly complex and culturally diverse. As diverse members of the worldwide body of Christ are able to communicate and meet more easily than ever before, many are realizing the great potential for mutual enrichment in the world church.

NEW TESTAMENT COMMUNITY, PUBLIC FAITH, AND THE POTENTIAL FOR MUTUAL ENRICHMENT

Many of the seven billion people alive on the planet today, including many of those living in Africa, would not be surprised at all by Dunbar's findings. Many of the cultures in the world still highly value the personal relationships of close communities. Christians from these parts of world, including East Africa, rejoice to see the emphasis on community life in the Bible. Traditional African community shares much in common with New Testament community. Asamoah-Gyadu (2015) describes how Pentecostalism emphasizes the work and power of the Holy Spirit to heal and deliver today as it did in biblical times in a way that resonates clearly with African spirituality and imagination. Many communities of the East African diaspora would agree with Asamoah-Gyadu (2015: 181) when he declares, "A church that flows in the power of the Spirit can never be an orphan." True community is a gift from the God who created life in community. God alone nurtures true community as we gather in the name of Christ and trust in the power of the Holy Spirit.

As the African Christian diaspora in the United States continues to grow, there are growing opportunities for Americans to learn from the witness and wisdom of these communities. These diaspora communities can teach American Christians new insights about biblical faith and community from a truly global perspective. They can teach others how God is at work in parts of the world where true evangelical awakenings and revivals still thrive today. In turn, American Christians can help African Christian diaspora communities adjust to life in a culture where true community can be culturally and logistically harder to find and maintain. Offutt (2015: 160) reminds us "a less distinctive religious community does not necessarily mean increased secularism." Many Kenyans and Tanzanians in diaspora remain committed to faith and community even in challenging diaspora contexts. In the process, many use social media in innovative and positive ways that build community and express public faith simultaneously. Together, Kenyan, Tanzanian, and American Christians can cooperate to develop and share new, more diverse Christian communities as well as new, grassroots public theologies that engage with and critique culture in innovative ways using the combined resources, wisdom, and capital of the world church.

Andrew Walls (1996: 54) reminds us, "It is a delightful paradox that the more Christ is translated into the various thought forms and life systems which form our various national identities, the richer all of us will be in our common Christian identity." Christians from diverse cultural backgrounds can share and learn from diverse and unique, spiritual and cultural gifts. At the same time, diverse members of the body of Christ are able to help one another see and address the cultural "blindspots" that exist in every one of our cultures. Walls (2002: 47) notes,

"Shared reading of the scriptures and shared theological reflection will be of benefit to all, but the oxygen-starved Christianity of the West will have the most to gain."

The Christian communities of the East African diaspora can not only teach Americans how to read the scriptures with fresh eyes but they can also help others rediscover and value true, New Testament community and hospitality. Pohl (2012: 161) reminds us, "Hospitality and shared meals fill the pages of scripture." Embracing this biblical teaching and early Christian tradition, African led-congregations both in Africa and in diaspora value hospitality and shared meals as well. Mungure (2011: 442-443) emphasizes how Christians from East Africa value sharing meals and stories as integral parts of prayer and worship in ways that help us remember the Eucharist. As we gather in the name of Christ to share meals and stories of faith, Christ is present within our homes as well as in our churches.

For many Christians from East Africa living in diaspora, invitations to share meals and stories with their American neighbors in their homes, help to create essential social, cultural and spiritual capital far from home. Shortly after arriving in the United States, my (Reuben) family "often shared meals with friends where we could fellowship and share our stories of living and ministering in Kenya as they shared their stories of living in the United States. As I reflect, I believe it was through sharing of our life stories that good friendships began to be formed" (Lang'at 2015).

If this sharing of meals and life stories does not take place, "mutual suspicion and ignorance" (Adogame 2013: 207) can plague relations between African diaspora communities and their host communities in Europe and America. Genuine Christian hospitality marked by the willingness to truly listen is crucial in preventing and overcoming the ignorance that creates suspicion. While music and shared meals are essential, genuine partnerships and fellowship must go far beyond and "transcend the frequent parading of African choirs of African food cultures" (Adogame 2013: 207). We will all benefit if we strive to "extend hospitality to others, be open to hearing people's stories, be obedient to Christ, and partner with brothers and sisters from other parts of the world to further the kingdom of Christ" (Lang'at 2015).

Host and diaspora communities must be equally patient, open and flexible. All must be willing to listen and learn. All must be willing to speak and hear the truth in love, when necessary. True community involves sharing prayer concerns and the willingness to rejoice and mourn together. True spiritual capital involves the willingness to teach, correct and hold one another accountable in the name of Christ. This is one of the unique and important legacies of the East African Revival.

Christians in East Africa continue to write their own histories of the East Africa Revival and its ongoing influence and legacy. Now, members of the East African diaspora, which is still a very young diaspora, are presented the task of documenting and sharing their diaspora experience. They have their own stories to share. While these stories will include shared experiences of faith and migration, they will also include individual voices expressing deeply personal and honest reflections that remind us "we must avoid trying to put too firm a boundary around diaspora communities (i.e., essentializing their identities), seeing them rather as dynamic and changing communities interacting in complex sociocultural contexts in the host society as well as back home" (Ybarrola 2012: 92-93). Hopefully, this small study can inspire Christians from East Africa to continue sharing and writing down their stories and thoughtful self-analyses of diaspora life and public faith.

CONCLUSION

While Kenyans and Tanzanian Christians agree that Muhando's warnings about the abuses of social media, especially in their home contexts, are genuine and fair, most also realize that social media in itself is not bad if used properly. Those living in diaspora appreciate the power of social media to help them build and maintain true Christian community even when they are geographically isolated from family and friends scattered across continents. In Kenyan and Tanzanian diaspora communities, the social capital and the spiritual capital of the Christian community are intertwined and inseparable. Social media allows them to share prayer requests and pray with others anytime, anywhere. In diaspora, social media becomes an essential tool for Christians from Kenya and Tanzania who value the biblical call to rejoice and mourn together in community.

Religion still plays a major role in the lives of most Africans, including the highly educated members of diaspora communities. Kenyan and Tanzanian Christians were born and raised during a time of remarkable revival and church growth in East Africa and many seek to maintain core elements of their culture and faith as they live in diaspora. Many embrace the transnational practice of joining phone prayer groups that connect people across continents. This innovative use of social media, group prayer by phone, has emerged as a vital and unique African Christian diaspora phenomenon. Others use social media to share music and preaching that can inspire and encourage anyone in the world with access to the Internet. Others use social media to continue ministries of mercy, evangelism and pastoral care back in East Africa even while living in diaspora.

As Kenyans and Tanzanians in diaspora share their own stories, they also share their faith and trust in God's larger story. The prayers and testimonies that Kenyans and Tanzanians share on social media express a faith lived in public and visible to Facebook "friends" all over the globe. The self-portraits Kenyans and Tanzanians share on social media are ones that often show a faith that combines social and spiritual capital just as it combines private and public faith. Kenyan and Tanzanian Christian diaspora communities can help Americans rediscover biblical community and hospitality. The new and innovative ways in which these diaspora communities use social media demonstrate their desire to share a dynamic grassroots public theology as they live a public faith.

While Christians all over the world use social media in positive ways to maintain and energize faith in both home and diaspora contexts, many remember that we are called to biblical hospitality and community. Kenyans and Tanzanians understand that social media is ultimately a tool for inviting others to share meals and stories with them. Sometimes these stories must be shared across continents as scattered communities pray together over the phone, but these connections can still create essential social and spiritual capital. Life in Christ has always been life in community, modeled on life in the Triune God of community and fellowship. As the Holy Spirit continues to move, we must continue to research and document how Christians on the move today carry with them not just private faith but also the public faith of ongoing revivals as they cross borders, from new heartlands of the world church to old ones and back again. True hospitality and community will increase mutual understanding and help ensure that our private lives and faith match our public self-portraits and theologies on social media. In the process, we can help one another learn how to share our private faith in public and engage with increasingly diverse and interconnected cultures with a public faith that reflects both the ancient and contemporary wisdom of the world church in a rapidly changing world.

REFERENCE LIST

Adogame, Afe

2011 *Who is Afraid of the Holy Ghost?: Pentecostalism and Globalization in Africa and Beyond.* Trenton, NJ: Africa World Press.

2013 *The African Christian Diaspora: New Currents and Emerging Trends in World Christianity.* New York: Bloomsbury.

Asamoah-Gyadu, J. Kwabena

2013 *Contemporary Pentecostal Christianity: Interpretations from an African Context.* Eugene, OR: Wipf & Stock.

2015 *Sighs and Signs of the Spirit: Ghanaian Perspectives on Pentecostalism and Renewal in Africa.* Eugene, OR: Wipf and Stock.

Bauerlein, Mark

2011 *The Digital Divide: Arguments for and Against Facebook, Google, Texting and the Age of Social Networking.* New York: Jeremy P. Tarcher/Penguin.

Breslin, Sean

2015 "Selfie Deaths Have Outnumbered Shark Attack Deaths in 2015." Published: Sep 22 2015 12:00 AM EDT. weather.com https://weather.com/travel/news/selfies-shark-attacks-comparison?_escaped_fragment_.

Buchanan, Rose Troup

2015 "Facebook used by half the world's Internet users." Retrieved from http://www.independent.co.uk/life-style/gadgets-and-tech/facebook-used-by-half-the-worlds-internet-users-10426003 html 30 July 2015.

Capps, Randy, Kristen McCabe, and Michael Fix
 2011 *New Streams: Black African Migration to the United States.* Washington, DC: Migration Policy Institute.

Dufoix, Stephane
 2008 *Diasporas.* Berkeley: University of California Press.

Economist
 2016 "Done, bar the counting: Online Social networks do not change the fundamentals of friendship," Jan 23, 2016. *Social Science.* www.economist.com/news/science-and-technology/21688846-online-social-networks-do-not-change-fundamentals-friendship-done-bar.

Eriksen, Thomas H.
 2015 *Small Places, Large Issues: An Introduction to Social and Cultural Anthropology.* Fourth Edition. London: Pluto Press.

Gornik, Mark
 2011 *Word Made Global: Stories of African Christianity in New York City.* Grand Rapids, MI. Eerdmans.

Hanciles, Jehu
 2008 *Beyond Christendom: Globalization, Africa Migration, and the Transformation of the West.* Maryknoll. NY: Orbis.

Johnson, Todd M. and Kenneth R. Ross
 2009 *Atlas of Global Christianity: 1910-2010.* Ed. Todd M. Johnson and Kenneth R. Ross. Managing Editor Sandra S.K. Lee. Edinburgh: Edinburgh University Press.

Kalu, Ogbu
 2011 "Who is afraid of the Holy Ghost? Presbyterian and Early Charismatic Movement in Nigeria," in *Who is Afraid of the Holy Ghost?: Pentecostalism and Globalization in Africa and Beyond.* Ed. Afe Adogame, p. 83-110. Trenton, NJ: Africa World Press.

Keen, Andrew
 2012 *#Digital Vertigo: How today's online social revolution is dividing, diminishing, and disorienting us.* New York: St. Martin's Press.

Lang'at, Reuben
    2015   "Life between two cultures." In *The Lookout*, Nov. 2015, Vol. CXXVII. Number 44.

Ludwig, Freider and J. Kwabena Asamoah-Gyadu
    2011   *African Christian Presence in the West: New Immigrant Congregations and Transnational Networks in North America and Europe.* Trenton, NJ: Africa World Press.

Metz, Cade
    2016   "One Billion People Now Use WhatsApp" retrieved from http://www.wired.com/2016/02/one-billion-people-now-use-whatsapp.

Migration Policy Institute
    2015   "RAD Diaspora Profile: The Kenyan Diaspora in the United States." June 2015 Revised.

Miller, Grant
    2016   *"Uamsho, Uhuru na Umoja* (Revival, Freedom and Unity): The Transnational Faith and Identity of Tanzanian Christians Negotiating Diaspora Life in the United States." PhD dissertation, Asbury Theological Seminary.

Muhando, Rose
    2014   "Facebook." Kamata Pindo la Yesu. DVD. Msama Promotions. Dar es Salaam.

Mungure, Elieshi A.
    2011   "African Christianity and the Neo-Diaspora: A Call for Cross-cultural Pastoral Care Approach and its Challenges. Appendix 4." In *African Christian Presence in the West: New Immigrant Congregations and Transnational Networks in North America and Europe.* Ed. Freider Ludwig and J. Kwabena Asamoah-Gyadu, p. 439-450. Trenton, NJ: Africa World Press.

Nyang, S. S.

        The African Immigrant Family in the United States of America: Challenges and Oppotunites. Department of Africana Studies. Washington, DC: Howard University.

Retrieved from:
   http://www.africamigration.com/Issue%205/Articles/HTML
   /Sulayman-Nyang_The-African-Immigrant-in-the-USA.htm.

Offutt, Stephen
   2015   *New Centers of Global Evangelicalism in Latin America and
          Africa*. New York: Cambridge University Press.

Oliver, Roland
   1952   *The Missionary Factor in East Africa*. London: Longman,
          Green and Co. Ltd.

Palfrey, John and Urs Gasser
   2011   "Activists," in *The Digital Divide: Arguments for and Against
          Facebook, Google, Texting and the Age of Social Networking*. Ed.
          Mark Bauerlein, p. 189-206. New York: Jeremy P. Tarcher/
          Penguin.

Pohl, Christine D.
   2012   *Living into Community: Cultivating Practices that Sustain Us*.
          Grand Rapids, MI: Eerdmans.

Rosen, Christine
   2011   "Virtual friendship and the new narcissism," in *The Digital
          Divide: Arguments for and Against Facebook, Google, Texting
          and the Age of Social Networking*. Ed. Mark Bauerlein, p. 172-
          188. New York: Jeremy P. Tarcher/Penguin.

Russell, S., and Batchy
   2014   *Galatians 3:28 Beyond Status and Role: Living Anti-Structurally
          Within Structure*. Manuscript in Preparation.

Shaw, Mark
   2010   *Global Awakening: How 20th-century Revivals Triggered a
          Christian Revolution*. Downer's Grove, IL: IVP Academic.

Shirky, Clay
   2011   "Means" in *The Digital Divide: Arguments for and Against
          Facebook, Google, Texting and the Age of Social Networking*. Ed.
          Mark Bauerlein, p. 318-344. New York: Jeremy P. Tarcher/
          Penguin.

Stern, Aaron
>1979   *Me: The Narcissistic American.* New York: Ballantine Books.

Twenge, Jean M. and W. Keith Campbell
>2009   *The Narcissism Epidemic: Living in the Age of Entitlement.* New York: Free Press.

Terrazas, A.
>2009   *African Immigrant in the United States.* Migration Policy Institute. Retrieved from http://www.migrationpolicy.org/article/african-immigrants-united-states-0.

Walls, Andrew
>1996   *The Missionary Movement in Christian History: Studies in the Transmission of Faith.* Maryknoll, NY: Orbis Books.

>2002   *The Cross-Cultural Process in Christian History: Studies in the Transmission and Appropriation of Faith.* Maryknoll, NY: Orbis Books.

Walters K.and Auton-Cuff, F.
>2009   "A story to Tell: The Identity Development of Women Growing up as Third Culture Kids." *Mental Health, Religion & Culture*, 12 (7) (November): 755-772.

Wan, Enoch and Yaw Attah Edu-Bekoe
>2013   *Scattered Africans Keep Coming: A Case Study of Diaspora Missiology on Ghanaian Diaspora and Congregations in the USA.* Portland, OR: IDSUS.

Ward, Kevin
>1991   "Tukutendereza Yesu: The Balokole Revival in Uganda." In *Mission to Church: A Handbook of Christianity in East Africa.* Ed. Zablon Nthamburi. Nairobi, Kenya: Uzima Press.

Ward, Kevin and Emma Wildwood
>2010   *The East African Revival: History and Legacies.* Kampala, Uganda: Fountain Publishers.

Ward, Kevin, Manuel Maranga and Isaac Kawuki Mukasa
>2013   "The East African Revival and the Revitalization of Christianity." In *Revitalization amid Diaspora: Consultation Three: Explorations in World Christian Revitalization*

Movements. Ed. Steven O'Malley, p. 9-35. Lexington, KY: Emeth Press.

Ybarrola, Steven
    2012   "Anthropology, Diasporas, and Mission," *Mission Studies* 29: 79–94.

Mission as Dialogue for Peace-Building

Joanne Blaney, MKLM

DOI: 10.7252/Paper. 000078

I. Introduction - Mission experience and Challenges of the Gospel Message

Life in urban, poor neighborhoods raises many questions about the church's theology of mission as "Encounter and Dialogue for Justice and Peace-Building." The violent context in which many people live and their lack of faith in the formal justice system challenge us to examine new ways to proclaim the Gospel as a liberating force that fosters human dignity and converts hearts. I have always struggled with questions as to how to truly live gospel values in a world so torn apart by violence, poverty and injustice. In living and working as a Maryknoll Lay Missioner in São Paulo, Brazil for 18 years, I accompanied communities and, especially in the last 9 years, pastoral agents, staff, and inmates in the prison system.

Experiencing the deep spirituality and faith of many of the Brazilian people and seeing sinful structures up close lead me to reflect upon how we as a church and society respond to the call of the gospel to justice and right relationships, love, mercy, and reconciliation. Have we watered down the gospel to conform to structures that contribute to the marginalization of people and that lack the dialogue necessary for peace-building?

The news is full of stories of violence and exclusion, whether it is societal, political, or familial. We see how the cycle of violence is repeated where the victim of aggression, many times, becomes an offender in some way. This cycle is propagated by the media as well as other groups in their portrayal of a "strong" person as one who is harsh in judgement or takes revenge. Individual and collective traumas can lead to "an eye for an eye" or a sense of hopelessness. In some ways, we can see this in the current political process in the U.S. and other countries.

The gospel passages related to forgiveness and love of enemies and the example of the life of Jesus confront us with different values as to what it means to be strong. Luke 6: 37 exhorts us: "Do not judge and you will not be judged. Do not condemn and you will not be condemned. Forgive and you will be forgiven." The parable of the unmerciful servant in Matthew 18: 21-35 begins with the question: "Lord, how many times must I forgive my brother or sister who sins against me? Up to seven times?" Jesus answered, "I tell you, not seven times, but seventy-seven times."

What does missiology say to a situation where the majority of the population is Christian and many do not believe that forgiveness and justice are truly possible?

Missio Dei, God's presence and involvement in and with the world, compels us to work to change all that is not of the Gospel. In our daily mission work we saw instance after instance of injustice and exclusion in the neighborhood, school, and judicial system. The reality of daily life of so many people demands that they submit to "harshness," whether it be poverty, overcrowded buses, exclusion from social services or dealing with drug gangs and all kinds of violence. It is not enough to listen and console; we are called to work to change the structures that contribute to this reality and to find new ways to build peace. Jesus proclaimed and worked toward fundamental changes in the society of his day. David Bosch[1] reminds us of the ethical and social thrust of the transformative mission of Jesus as indicated in Luke 4:18: "The Spirit of the Lord is upon me, because he has anointed me to proclaim good news to the poor. He has sent me to proclaim freedom for the prisoners and recovery of sight for the blind, to set the oppressed free." How can we live out this message given the punishment and revenge model that is so rampant in our societies? Are there alternatives to this model?

II. Approach and Methodologies

At the Popular Education and Human Rights Center in São Paulo - Brazil, my colleagues and I developed a program "Forgiveness and Restorative Justice" so as to indicate that justice and forgiveness are not exclusive of each other and that they are achievable. The ministry approach that we applied was a *dialogical, participative process* that worked with real issues within the context of people's lives and experiences. One methodology used in the program is based on a process developed by the Fundación para la Reconciliación (Foundation for Reconciliation) in Bogota, Columbia. This process, ESPERE, or Schools of Forgiveness and Reconciliation, works with all kinds of communities and groups and is now in 15 countries. Its founder, Leonel Narvaez Gomez is a Consolata Missionary priest who worked with communities in Kenya and Colombia where

---

1   Bosch, David J. *Transforming Mission-Paradigm Shifts in Theology of Mission*, Maryknoll, New York: Orbis Books, 1991.

he saw the same dynamic of violence among nomadic rural tribes and urban groups in conflict.

ESPERE is a process that works to *deconstruct memories* based on narratives of hurt, anger, hatred, and revenge in a "safe" collective space so that these memories can be deconstructed. Through experiential encounters and reflection, another narrative can be constructed, one that includes a new way of seeing others and the world. This healing and experience of community opens participants up to catharsis, a change of heart, which can lead to empathy and forgiveness.

Components of Restorative Justice

My colleagues and I built upon this process and added concepts and practices of Restorative Justice. In contrast to the current retributive model of punishment, Restorative Justice proposes a different way of responding to wrongdoing.

a.   It focuses on who has been harmed and how best to repair this harm.

b.   It is concerned with restoring victims and the community to a healthy state.

c.   It begins with the offender taking responsibility for an action and gives space for the victim to speak about the effect of the conflict/crime in his/her life.

d.   Restorative Justice works for rehabilitation of the offender and the process includes all of those affected by the conflict.

e.   It focuses on truth-telling which includes individual and *collective responsibility.*

f.   Circles take place in a community setting and the hope is for reintegration of the victim and offender and all involved in the conflict. Through respectful dialogue, peace can be built.

Our program "Forgiveness and Restorative Justice" helps participants to rethink and rebuild concepts of "forgiveness," "truth," and "justice." Our experience shows us that most people are dissatisfied with the punishment-vengeance model but don't see another way to bring about a just-justice for all in a non-violent way. The fact that we use the term "just-justice" indicates how pervasive is the belief by many that "true justice" cannot and does not take place. Many times, we heard,

"I don't believe in justice" or "Only God can forgive." Our experience with folks who live in vulnerable situations illustrates the importance of self-forgiveness/forgiveness and a real justice process so that they are not paralyzed by guilt, blame, anger, and/or hatred. *Spirituality* is an integral part of the program and interwoven in it. In respectful encounters that recognize the human dignity of each person, borders are crossed that lead to an experience of our interconnectedness with each other, which many times leads to empathy and compassion. This "conversion of heart" comes from a real-life experience and process and not only from reading and reflection. An experience of seeing the other as truly my brother or sister helps people move forward in life and break free from the cycle of violence.

We worked on this program with educators, social workers, NGOs, youth, church groups, diocesan priests, inmates, and the prison pastors throughout Brazil. Participants in our program commit to becoming "multipliers" of forgiveness and restorative justice and, where possible, *work to change unjust public policies.* This is an important aspect of our program, a recognition that there is *individual responsibility but also collective responsibility* of the state and social service projects, especially in regards to treatment of adolescent offenders or adult inmates who live horrific conditions.

III. Case studies and their Connections to Christian Values and Missiological Concepts

I will now present a brief vignette of five case studies:

Case One: Working with one's own anger and grief

Renata and Andrea are two young women who were deeply traumatized by their father's murder on the streets of São Paulo. Both women stopped participating in their Church community because of their inability to truly pray the phrase of the "Our Father – forgive us our trespasses as we forgive others." Their suffering was compounded by their experience of guilt in feeling rage and a desire for revenge for the perpetrator. Both women found themselves estranged from their own family and the community. Renata had worked as a catechist and, in her words, "My life became a torment." The Forgiveness and Restorative Justice process helped her to elaborate and work with her anger and grief. Today, Renata is a different person, very involved in her community and a coordinator of a children's project that teaches them the forgiveness and justice process. In her words, "Learning to forgive gave me back my life. I want to help others escape this horrible cycle of violence and revenge."

Case Two: Dialogical encounter with the other

Dona Cida's only son was murdered as he was returning home from work. In a neighborhood where very few crimes are investigated, Dona Cida's grief was overwhelming in the face of this senseless killing. She wanted answers to her son's death. The police and her own family pressured her to "leave it alone…it is better not to know." Dona Cida met the young man arrested for the death of her son and learned from him that he had been robbed of important work documents and thought that it was her son who stole them. It was a case of mistaken identity. He begged for forgiveness. In Dona Cida's words: "In that moment, I saw another young man just like my son and was able to forgive." It was through this forgiveness process that Dona Cida indicates that she was later able to stop her son's friends from taking revenge, stating that "This will not bring back the life of my son." Dona Cida's decision to choose compassion happened in a dialogical encounter with "the other," an encounter where respect, responsibility, and compassion were born. Today, she is a community leader in a neighborhood social project.

Case Three: Breaking down the image of "the other"

Bia and Paulo are adolescents who were involved in an incident of cyberbullying. The case centered on the deep hurt and anger of Bia, the young girl who suffered from a video posted on Youtube. Her mother, Diana, reported the incident to a number of police stations in the hope that Paulo would be arrested and made to "suffer greatly for what he did….locked up forever." Diana had created an image of Paulo as a "horrible monster" who "should never be forgiven and can await the greatest punishment from God." In the restorative process, Diana and Bia came to see him as a young man who admitted his error, accepted responsibility for his action and desired to repair the harm in some way. The encounter broke down the "image of the other" and changed Diana's focus on punishment and revenge as the way to deal with this conflict. It even led to a sense of solidarity and community among the family participants. In Diana's words, "I can now move on." Bia herself stated, "I feel so relieved that this is over. I feel like a weight was lifted from me."

Case Four: Hearing the other's story

Victor is an adolescent arrested for a car-hijacking. After completing time in a juvenile detention center, he encountered Raquel, the victim of the hijacking, by chance in the neighborhood. We wo rked with him to begin a restorative justice process. Raquel agreed to the process and stated that "Even knowing that Victor was punished, I felt no peace. I wanted to know why this happened to me." The results of the process are summed up in Raquel's final words:

"I believe in change and that you, Victor, have your whole life in front of you. Hearing your story, I believe that you were more of a victim in this perverse system of punishment. Today has helped me to overcome this trauma. Go after your life and search for a new story. It would be good if your mother were here so that she could be proud of you, of your courage to come here today. Your courage brought me here today. I even want to participate in your new story. I invite you to register at our school."

Case Five: Collective responsibility

Staff of a school where a young child drowned were traumatized. The teacher accused of negligence left the school immediately after the young child was found, stating that "my life is over." However, in the process, it became clear that there were many others with some responsibility: those who took the fence down surrounding the lake where the child drowned, those who complained about it but said nothing, the assistant teacher who was also not present with the children, etc. This sense of collective responsibility is key to our process. In retributive justice, individual responsibility is the focus. In varied cases, including this one, it became clear that the teacher alone was not individually responsible. The child's grandmother was a staff member of the school and was a key figure in the forgiveness and restorative process. When her adult sons wanted to burn down the school she was able to pacify them, "This will not bring back my grandchild." In some way, those who participated in the process were able to cross over the borders that divided them from each other and to see in the eyes of the other a mirror of themselves.

The cases illustrate how *"mission as encounter" can heal hurt, anger, and hatred.* A grace or energy bigger than the individuals is created that helps compassion to be reborn. The transformations that took place among the community members involved in these processes were hopeful. Participants talked about how they understood justice, truth, and forgiveness in a new way. Members helped to integrate the victim and offender back into the community. Repair of the harm was decided among those involved in the conflict and reintegration of all was a priority. The "offenders," many times, commented that "in this process they felt respected and could really tell the truth about the situation." No one was advising them to "plead innocent and not say anything." As one inmate at a woman's prison asked, "With this process, I don't have to lie in front of the judge?" Offenders also talked about how, with this process, they could *see the impact of what they had done, work to repair the harm* and have community support to move forward with their lives.

The "victims" talked about how light they felt after being able to share their pain with the person who caused it. Doing this, and knowing that the other has listened and wants to repair the harm in some way helps victims to be able to see the other as a human being who also has a story. One victim whose son was murdered was advised by others to be harsh and unforgiving, exacting in demanding punishment. She commented that when she met the offender's mother, "In that moment, I saw someone who was just like me, poor, hard-working, and trying to do her best for her children."

Extended Forgiveness and Restorative Justice Training in Alternative Community Settings

All of us face ordinary life traumas and, many times, carry a heaviness in our heart and soul. These unresolved hurts and angers can cause a lack of compassion and solidarity. In addition to formal restorative processes, we have given courses and workshops to all kinds of groups (homeless people, priests and ministers, local neighborhood groups, etc.) Our experience shows that the path to forgiveness and a "just" justice that restores people is attractive to many in our world today. These processes are not easy but they tap into people's dissatisfaction and sadness with the status quo. The focus on collective responsibility has helped us to foster the use of these practices in public institutions as well. This is an uphill battle. As Murilo, a state public prosecutor, stated, "This course has shown me a new way to deal with violence. Along with theory, it deals with lived experiences of us as individuals and expands to the collective, showing how dealing with violence can and should occur in the public sphere. As a result of this formation, we now have proposals for changes in public policy related to crime, prisons, and adolescent offenders." As the staff member of a prison in São Paulo stated, "I want to participate in this process of Forgiveness and Restorative Justice. I've seen the change in these men (inmates)." Other comments include this statement by Ricardo: "I was a very vengeful person. I learned this from my family. I am now an inmate in this prison because of what I did. In this course, I learned that violence and revenge are not the answer. I'd like to repair the harm that I caused in some way." Seu José, a 78 year old inmate in a prison said: "I wouldn't be here today had I known earlier what I learned and experienced here."

I believe that the Gospel calls us to work to *create communal environments* where each person is respected, has a voice and is listened to by others. Part of our work includes the creation of a safe space where small groups of people grapple with what they have suffered and done, no matter how large or small. This first step in building a "community" is healing and empowering. It helps to deconstruct hopelessness and, at the same time, awakens energy to move forward in life. What transforms human hearts? The Gospel mandate to love includes the hallmarks of forgiveness, conversion, and inclusion.

IV. Concluding Statements

Raimon Pannikar speaks of "*dialogical dialogue*" that leads to recognizing difference but also points to what we have in common, which in the end produces mutual fecundation. Dialogue, for him, is not a "luxury for humankind, it is something absolutely necessary…a deep-reaching human dialogue that is a joint search since wisdom consists in being able to listen."[2] In our work with "Forgiveness and Restorative Justice," the outcome is unknown. However, the soil in these methodologies is fertile soil for expression, listening, and dialogue. Pannikar reminds us that, "Life is a risk; adventure is radical innovation; creation comes about day after day, it is something absolutely new and unforeseeable."[3] Out of pain and suffering can come hope, the hope that is born in encounters that can lead to a liberating process for all. This, to me, is a big part of the heart of mission: to proclaim a God of life to transform the world by the building up of, in Pope Paul VI's words, a civilization of love.

---

2   Raimon Pannikar. *Mística comparada?* Madrid: VVAA La mística en el siglo XXI, 2002.
3   Raimon Pannikar. *Cultural Disarmament: The Way to Peace*, Westminster: Knox Press, 1995.

The experience of the mysterious Divine can be seen in each of these processes where compassion was born through solidarity and recognition that we are all brothers and sisters. Walls that divided human beings from each other were crossed in a way that followed the parables and storytelling of Jesus. Truth is seen as more than just the "cold facts" but is rather experienced in the way of Jesus who saw much more in Mary Magdalen or Zaccheus, the tax collector. *A grace or presence bigger than the individual parts* allowed compassion and forgiveness (what is not "logically possible") to be born. This "inbreaking of God's reign of mercy and justice and reconciliation recognizes the dignity and the tragedy of the human person. It is always an invitation to a faith community."[4]

As a Maryknoll Lay Missioner whose mission vision is to help to create a more just and compassionate world, I truly believe that I have seen the birth of real justice and compassion in this work. Something sacramental happens in the process and "metanoia" can happen for all involved. I have heard a victim state in the beginning of the process, "I will never forgive. This person will pay dearly for what they have done." The final agreement was one of restored relationships, forgiveness, and repair of the harm. Perhaps it truly is possible to taste on earth a bit of the vision of Isaiah 6:

> "Then the wolf shall be a guest of the lamb, and the leopard shall lie down with the young goat; the calf and the young lion shall browse together."

With increased levels of violence and conflict in our world, may we take risks to create anew the Gospel message in light of the harsh reality for so many people in our world. May our eyes be opened to see that, in the words of Pope Francis, "God's mercy can make even the driest land become a garden, can restore life to dry bones (cf. Ez 37:1-14). ... Let us be renewed by God's mercy... let us become agents of this mercy, channels through which God can water the earth, protect all creation and make justice and peace flourish."[5] May we participate in a mission of dialogue in order to support actions for human flourishing and to build peace!

---

4   Pope Francis. *Easter Urbi et Orbi Message*, Vatican, 2013.
5   Pope Francis. *Easter Urbi et Orbi Message*, Vatican, 2013.

Faith and Politics:

Rwanda, a Case History

BOB RICE

DOI: 10.7252/Paper. 000079

"You have heard that bishops were killed, priests were killed, Christians suffer, but *the church lives*. Satan is jealous because there were so many Christians in the country," Archbishop Augustin Nshamihigo of Rwanda tells his Afro-Anglican colleagues after leaving Rwanda for (former) Zaire and eventually Nairobi. The devil has retaliated with pain and death in Rwanda due to *the success* of the church, elaborates Nshamihigo.[1] The 1994 genocide in Rwanda claimed the lives of more than eight hundred thousand men, women and children. The genocidal war-machine mobilized and slaughtered people at a higher rate than that of Nazi Germany. Satan, as Nshamihigo surmises, is the easy target regarding such cataclysmic evil.

Yet, what should we infer from Nshamihigo's comment regarding the devil retaliating because of the Church's "success?" Gary Sheer, a missionary to Rwanda, questions the 'success' of the Church in Rwanda in his article "Rwanda: Where was the church?"[2] After the genocide, Sheer understandably ponders what influence the church should have had to countermand such vitriolic evil. Why did the Church seemingly fail at such a critical hour? Sheer believes that we must now ponder, question, and wrestle regarding the church and what happened. What can we learn today from the Church in Rwanda? In this paper I will argue that the Christian faith must govern "all of life" and can find its entry point through the social/economic/political aspirations of its people. To accomplish this task, I will address the historical background of Rwanda. I will then highlight the significant role of the East African Revival upon the Rwandan Church, celebrating its strengths but more importantly (for this paper), citing its deficiencies. I will address the controversial but highly significant role of politics as it relates to the Christian faith, also discussing the Church's mission of justice and love. I will conclude with the need for the Church of Rwanda to repent of her shame and failure to the people of Rwanda.

Rwanda is comprised of three people groups: Twa, Hutu, Tutsi. These three groups lived together for centuries, sharing the same language and culture. The Twa are believed to have been the first people to live in the region of Rwanda. Of pygmoid background, they generally lived in the forests and hunted for animals. The Hutu, the majority of the population, traditionally cultivated the soil. The Hutu

---

1   Jeanie Wylie-Kellerman, "Differing Views on Rwanda," *The Witness*, Volume 78, Number 6, June 1995, pg. 14. Italics mine.

2   Gary Sheer, "Rwanda: Where was the church?" *Evangelical Missions Quarterly*, Volume 31, No. 3, July 1995, pgs. 326 – 328.

resemble the peoples of Uganda and Tanzania. The Tutsi were known for cattle herding. Most scholars speculate that they arrived in Rwanda somewhere between the twelfth and fifteenth centuries from Ethiopia. Europeans in the late nineteenth century romantized these three groups. The Twa were considered lowly, described as similar to the apes whom they chased in the forest. The Hutu were described as simple people who liked to laugh and were generally short in stature. The Tutsi were considered as superior beings, characterized as tall, thin, intelligent, refined, capable of incredible self-control, of goodwill, and as natural leaders.

These European characterizations of the Hutu, Tutsi and Twa had a profound impact upon the *Banyarwanda*[3] people themselves. For sixty years of colonial rule, the Tutsi self-identity was inflated while the Hutu identity was crushed.[4] Gerard Prunier, author of *The Rwanda Crisis, History of a Genocide* concludes,

> If we combine these subjective feelings with the objective political and administrative decisions of the colonial authorities favouring one group over the other, we can begin to see how a very dangerous social bomb was almost absent-mindedly manufactured throughout the peaceful years of *abazungu* [white] domination.[5]

Thus, we find that the racially obsessed Europeans of the late nineteenth and early twentieth century built an artificial construct of the Rwandan people which governed their relations with them. This construct was even exploited by adept Rwandans.

Socially, the early white explorers were struck by the significance of kingship. The *mwami* (king, always a Tutsi) lived at the center of the royal court and was treated as a divine being. The king had power over life and death. Yet, as Prunier contends, he was only the apex of a large and complex pyramid of political, economic, and social relationships.[6] Social mobility was possible through the institution of "*ubuhake*," whereby a Hutu (lower class) could work for a Tutsi (higher class) in exchange for a cow.[7] A Hutu could actually become a Tutsi if he gained

---

3   *Banyarwanda* is the term used for the people of Rwanda in their mother tongue, *Ikinyarwanda*.

4   I have not included the Twa here as the main focus of "ethnic rivalry" was between the Tutsi and the Hutu. The Twa were looked down upon by both groups.

5   Gerard Prunier, *The Rwanda Crisis, History of a Genocide*, Columbia University Press, New York, 1995. pg. 9.

6   Prunier, 12.

7   Cows serve as the primary source of wealth in traditional Rwandan society. If there is famine, a cow will help a family survive for a longer duration.

enough cattle; thus, social boundaries were permeable. Moreover, war served as a "social coagulant" for the *Banyarwanda* (Hutu, Tutsi, Twa) and *Kubandwa* cult religion also brought the three groups together.[8]

As Africa was carved up by European powers in the late nineteenth century, Germany was given authority over the region of Rwanda. Germans were somewhat laissez-faire in their approach and basically ruled through the king. German presence was short-lived as Rwanda was transferred to Belgian control in 1916. Belgian authority was different from that of Germany in that Belgium *cared*. While Rwanda was just a small area and ill-considered by the Germans, Belgium was pleased with her new African colony and sought to develop her. The Belgians favored the Tutsi and worked with them to control the society. Thus, Tutsi were given favor and privilege. The Hutu, conversely, suffered under a cruel forced labor system. The Belgians tightened the formerly porous social boundaries as a means of "divide and rule."

Though Christian conversion initially grew slowly in the 1920s in Rwanda with converts coming from the margins of society, Christianity became like "a white man's *ubuhake* system" to those who sought conversion.[9] The astute Tutsi realized that to survive changes set by the white man, it behooved them to convert to the Christian faith. Thus, a massive wave of converts flooded the Catholic Church. The Belgian authorities and religious leaders deposed King Musinga in 1931, replacing him with one of his sons, Mutara III Rudahigwa. Rudahigwa eventually converted to Christianity and would consecrate his country to Christ the King. Thus, writes Tharcisse Gatwa, a journalist from Rwanda and author of the article "Victims or Guilty," this event illustrates perfectly the marriage between Church and Crown.[10]

By 1932 the Catholic Church became the main social institution of Rwanda, overseeing hundreds of thousands of Rwandan converts. The Catholic Church had a monopoly on education, thus providing the means to develop an integrated and highly developed administrative apparatus. Yet, as Prunier deftly intuits, "Rwandese society under the influence of the church became if not truly virtuous, then at least conventionally hypocritical."[11] Shrewdly, Rwandans played the role the colonizers

8   Prunier, 15.
9   Prunier, 31.
10   Tharcisse Gatwa, "Victims or Guilty? Can the Rwandan Churches Repent and Bear the Burden of the Nation for the 1994 Tragedy?," *International Review of Mission*, Volume 88, 1999, pg. 356.
11   Prunier, 32.

wished them to play, mostly for their own survival. Reasons for conversion were basically social and political. Thus, in many ways true Christianity did not penetrate deeply into the hearts and minds of the Rwandese people.

Social and political winds began to change after 1945. As Belgian administration pushed the Rwandan people into individual economic agents, this drive led to independent thinking. Control of the church was slipping from white control as the Tutsi were beginning to embrace ideas such as ethnic equality and self-government;[12] these themes posed a tremendous threat to their Belgian overlords. As social relationships became grimmer, the Catholic Church began to favor the growth of a Hutu counter-elite. Furthermore, the leadership in the Belgian clergy was changing, reflecting more humble social origins which sympathized with the suppressed Hutu majority. The Hutu slowly began to organize themselves into societies and organizations, now feeling support from the Catholic Church.[13] Against all odds, notes Tharsisse Gatwa, the colonial officials and the Catholic Church converted to the Hutu cause. Gatwa believes this change had less to do with the new outlook of the Catholic clergy and was based more upon political motivations, namely the Church's desire to maintain a position of domination.[14] Regardless, this change in allegiance eventually led to the infamous "social revolution" of 1959 which changed the entire social and political landscape of Rwanda, inaugurating waves of open hostility between Hutu and Tutsi which dominated all aspects of life for the next forty years and culminated in the 1994 genocide.

In the midst of these political rivalries and dubious motives regarding conversion to the Christian faith, there shone a strong and powerful light which cannot be overlooked. In the 1930s, the fires of revival were strong and powerful throughout East Africa, starting in Gahini, Rwanda, and emanating outward. Pioneer missionaries and inquisitive Africans sought a deeper level of holiness. They sought to "walk in the light," living holy and devout lives. This movement became popularly known as the East African Revival. The Revival lasted for many years and resurfaced in the 1960s and 1970s. In a journal article written about the East African Revival, Richard Gehman remarks that this revival is one of the most remarkable movements of the Holy Spirit in the Christian Church.[15] The Revival

---

12   Prunier, 41 - 43.
13   Prunier, 45.
14   Gatwa, 357.
15   Richard Gehman, "The East African Revival," *East African Journal of Evangelical Theology*, 5 no. 1, 1986, pgs. 36 – 56.

spread through Rwanda and Uganda into neighboring countries and changed thousands of lives. People were transformed and began living highly moral lives. Denominations marked by nominal faith were deeply affected. This movement remained vital fifty years after its inception.[16]

The East African Revival had many strengths. It did not become a separate movement but remained within the churches. It was evangelical and evangelistic. It broke down walls between Hutu and Tutsi. It promoted lay involvement. It was noted for strong fellowship. Jocelyn Murray, in her case study of the East African Revival, positively notes that missionaries and Africans were on equal terms; both were concerned with personal holiness.[17] Dr. Noel Quinton (N.Q.) King, professor of religious studies at Makerere University College in Uganda, stressed the "overwhelmingly important" fact that this movement was a joint effort between both Africans and Europeans.[18] He commended the indigenous nature of the movement, possessing an African particularity. In churches dominated by Europeans, Africans were able to demonstrate leadership and exhibit their ability to maintain even higher standards than their European counterparts. King recognized the Revival's potential to "save the day in East Africa."[19]

While the East African Revival helped people live holy lives, it did not emphasize the role of faith in the public/political arena. This theme was its major deficiency. Although it broke down ethnic walls, it lacked a strong social engagement to justice and concern for those unjustly treated. Looking back after the 1994 genocide, one church elder confesses that none of the churches condemned the massacres.[20] Mugemera, a Rwandan pastor, admits to the shame of the church. The church in Rwanda lost its prophetic mission. Church leaders had become "sycophants to the authorities." No one from the churches had spoken against the violence from 1959 onward.[21] Antoine Rutayisire, a Rwandan Anglican pastor and former Team Leader of African Evangelistic Enterprise (AEE) Rwanda, directs

---

16   Gehman, 36.

17   Jocelyn Murray, "The East African Revival: A Case Study," *Conrad Grebel Review* 15 Winter/Spring 1997, pgs. 62 – 68.

18   Noel Quinton King, "The East African Revival Movement and Evangelism," *Ecumenical Review* 20 April 1968, pgs. 152 – 162.

19   King, 162.

20   Hugh McCullum, *The Angels Have Left Us, The Rwandan Tragedy and the Churches*, WCC Publications, Geneva, 1995. pg. 73.

21   McCullum, pg. 75.

blame at the church for seeing trouble brewing but doing nothing; the church, he says, even consented to and participated in ethnic division and hostility.[22]

Why was the church so thoroughly impotent in the face of ethnic animosity and tension? Was the message of personal holiness emphasized by missionary revivalist Joe Church and his African counterparts in the 1930s enough? Antoine says no. While he believes that the Revival rightly attacked social vices such as theft, drunkenness, adultery, jealousy, etc., it did so at the expense of social issues which were considered outside the sphere of God's grace.[23] Meg Guillebaud, a third generation missionary in Rwanda, writes in her book *Rwanda, The Land God Forgot?* that early missionaries discouraged Rwandans from getting involved in public life due to the fear of corruption. Missionaries at that time were heirs to a theological controversy which led them to emphasize evangelism rather than public engagement, being critical of social/political involvement.[24]

Roger Bowden, then General Secretary of Mid-Africa Ministry (MAM) of the Church Mission Society (CMS) stated in his J.C. Jones Lecture in 1995 that Rwanda had operated with a "privatized" and inadequate view of sin. He stipulated that the Revival doctrine of sin underestimated the depth and power of sin in its structural and corporate nature.[25] Robert Walker, writing for the BBC, wonders whether the church deserves more culpability after the 1994 cataclysm. The church hierarchy not only failed to denounce dissemination of ethnic hatred but even supported the regime which ultimately exacted suffering of such mammoth proportions.[26] As Bowden concludes, the personal and private nature of sin as understood from the Revival didn't prepare the church to corporately stand against evil structures within the government and the larger society. The church in its infancy and immaturity didn't understand that it possessed a prophetic voice to speak out. Those who applaud early missionary endeavors also stand in consternation after the 1994 Rwanda genocide. It seems that while the East African Revival emphasized personal holiness and simple faith, it lacked a more fully orbed theology which

---

22 Carl Lawrence, *Rwanda, A walk through darkness...into light*, Vision House Publishing, Inc., Gresham, OR, 1995. pg. 137.
23 Lawrence, pg. 138.
24 Meg Guillebaud, *Rwanda, The Land God Forgot?*, *Revival, Genocide and Hope*, Monarch Books, Grand Rapids, MI, 2002, pgs. 323 – 324.
25 Guillebaud, 323.
26 Robert Walker, Rwanda's religious reflections, BBC Kigali, http://news.bbc.co.uk/2/hi/africa/3561365.stm, 4/20/07.

would have equipped the Church to stand tall and speak out, countermanding the vitriol of ethnic rivalry.

With the East African Revival, Rwandans were authentically changed by the Gospel. It was more than the facade. Something deep and meaningful *had* transpired in the hearts and minds of thousands of Rwandans from the 1930s onward. When Archbishop Augustin Nshamihigo referred to the "success" of the church in Rwanda, he may have been alluding to the legacy of the East African Revival. He may also have been alluding to the high percentage of Rwandans who confessed Christianity as their religion.[27] Yet, others are less convinced about the "success" of the church. The obvious question must now be offered, how could genocide happen in such a "Christianized" country?

From the historical perspective, there is an easy explanation. The Catholic Church (in particular, but not alone) permitted and enabled nominal Christianity. The Rwandan population was keen enough to understand that conversion to the Church meant opportunity, financial and otherwise. Christianity in this sense was essentially superficial. Worse, the Church sided with those in positional places of power. Originally they worked with the Tutsi, but when political winds changed they sided with the Hutu. Although they seemed to have created a model "Christian nation" in the heart of Africa, this "model" turned into a nightmarish hell for the Rwandan people. "Where was the Church in 1994?" asks Gary Sheer and so many others. The Church was present, but it wasn't triumphant. While we cannot expect perfection this side of eternity, we can hope for a Church that reflects the character of God regarding justice, mercy, and love. Wolfgang Schonecke, addressing the Rwandan tragedy to the AMECEA Churches of East Africa, writes that the Rwandan experience poses urgent questions regarding the model of Church in Africa inherited from missionaries. He cites the lack of rootedness of the Church to Rwandan culture. He postulates a need for "radical inculturation."[28] But what does this "radical inculturation" look like and what does it mean?

For starters, Christianity must govern "all of life." One significant area of life it must be in relation with is the social/political arena. Politics is a pervasive reality. Economic and social structures are largely governed by politics. We find this

---

27 Most figures put this number at 90%, with 65% Catholic and 25% Protestant.
28 Fr. Wolfgang Schonecke, "What Does the Rwanda Tragedy Say to AMECEA Churches?", *AMECEA Documentation Service*, ADS 17/1994, No. 424. September 15th, 1994. pg. 6.

evident in the Rwanda story. The political influence of Belgium drastically altered the social and economic structures and even the very fiber of Rwandan society. Belgian political and administrative domination affected how Rwandans felt about the Christian religion. In his article "Politics and theology in Africa," Laurenti C. Magesa maintains that political systems strongly determine economic, social and even religious structures in Africa. These elements are all closely linked. Thus, contends Magesa, political realities should be central to doing theology as politics pervades human life.[29]

This notion finds biblical precedent. When Jeremiah spoke his highly unpopular prophetic message to Judah, he referred to the very real political realities which threatened to undo their nation. The Gospels make us aware of the political world Jesus faced during his earthly ministry. The region of Galilee was ruled by Herod the Tetrarch under the imperial jurisdiction of Rome. When Jesus spoke of the cross, one cannot doubt that he had seen crosses litter the landscape to remind the Jewish people the punishment that would befall them if they rebelled. Paul benefited politically in being a Roman citizen. He could travel freely and he was exonerated due to his citizenship status. He appealed to the higher governing authorities when he was in a bind. Political situations have had a definitive influence upon the Church. Early persecution sparked theological understanding of what it means to live and *die* for Christ. Thus, political situations make up a significant factor in the life of the Church and theological thought.[30]

Today, a concern dominating African theology is the inculturation of the Gospel.[31] Magesa believes that evangelism must be done *ad modum recipientis*, that is, it must consider the cultural context of its recipients. Understanding culture must be rooted within the complex web of socio-political-religious relationships. Although culture cannot be reduced to political systems, politics, understood as that which regulates human relationships, is the principle which unites and underlies all other areas of life in the world.[32] Thus,

> the political aspect or principle of life in Africa today, offers easier
> access to comprehending the socio-cultural, economic and religious

29   Laurenti C. Magesa, "Politics and theology in Africa," *African Ecclesial Review*, 31, 1989/3, pg. 147. When this article was written, Laurenti Magesa was a lecturer in Moral Theology at the Catholic Higher Institute of Eastern Africa (CHIEA).
30   Magesa, 148.
31   Magesa, 146.
32   Magesa, 147.

aspects. It is ... a more direct and relevant source of apposite theology, theology germane to today's African needs, demands, and expectations, particularly since independence.[33]

Politics is a critical entry point for theology in Africa. Christianity must be understood as more than just a private faith or a quest for personal holiness. Jesus came preaching the Kingdom of God. This Kingdom seeks the well-being of people and strives towards justice and love. Jesus' mission was to bring good news to the poor, to proclaim release to those in bondage, to bring sight to the blind, to set the oppressed free, and to proclaim God's goodness and mercy (Luke 45: 18 – 19). These actions have political import. Though Jesus was not a political revolutionary per se, his revolution of love and justice encompassed all of life which includes the political realm. Thus, when he began to upset the powers and structures of his day, particularly as he challenged the temple system (Luke 19: 45 – 47), he suffered a political death on the cross at the hands of the Romans by means of the connivance of the Jewish religious leaders. "The greatest moments of the history of salvation," writes Magesa, "are significantly set within the political context."[34] The politics of the Kingdom of God which Jesus embodied crashed head on with the politics of Israel and Rome. As Magesa deduces, the political dimension of the Kingdom of God will inevitably impinge upon the politics of the (secular) State.[35]

Has Africa taken seriously its politics as a source of theology? Does the Church understand its role on a continent riddled with political upheaval, poverty, tribalism, AIDS, war, debt, fear and a perpetual sense of hopelessness? The Church of Africa has a wonderful opportunity to show that Christianity is concerned with "all of life" and that God works in the midst of any political/social/economic reality. African theology should act as a "conscience moving factor,"[36] influencing all members of society to refuse cruelty and oppression in all spheres of life. Although the Kingdom of God and the Church are not equivalent in nature, the Church's role is to be the primary agent of God's Kingdom. Thus, the role of the Church is to bring freedom from oppression in all spheres of life: social, economic, political.

Members of the revival fellowship from the East African Revival did not see their role as one of repairing or reconstructing the fabric of society. Rather,

---

33   Magesa, 151.
34   Magesa, 146.
35   Magesa, 152.
36   Magesa, 158.

they saw themselves as members of a new community which would be a prophetic witness to the larger society. These dear brothers and sisters are not alone in their theological perspective. Different Christian groups throughout history have distanced themselves from "secular society," desiring to call others into their experience that transcends ordinary cultural, socio-economic and tribal barriers. While indeed this viewpoint has New Testament precedence, I agree with John Vernon Taylor, author of *Christianity and Politics in Africa*, that it is only part of the truth. Taylor contends that Christianity divorced from the overall developing life of the community will never do for Africa. Separation between Church and society goes against African tradition and sentiment where all of life is bound up together. Furthermore, it would be disastrous for those who are politically aware to disassociate themselves from the Church. Christianity is as concerned with the things of this world as with the things to come.[37]

George Ernest Wright, author of *The Biblical Doctrine of Man in Society*, agrees. "Our responsibility," he writes, "is in the here and now, and there must be no evasion of it."[38] Furthermore, he elucidates that the Christian's responsibility is to have an active, responsible, and positive role in the life of the world.[39] Joseph Fison makes the interesting observation that the Christian faith is a "materialistic faith." Embodied man has met with embodied God and with embodied nature. He argues against the "pie in the sky when you die" mentality.[40] While an eschatological hope in the renewal of all things is healthy for Christian life and witness, Fison's point regarding the "physicality" and the "earthiness" of our faith is significant. He heeds us to take stock of Hugel's warning to not become so enamored with grace that we despise nature (the here and now).[41]

Taylor elaborates that God calls men and women; he doesn't call "souls." God calls us to be responsible for our communities, to proactively shape the events of history, and to pattern society according to the laws of His Kingdom. God's Kingdom and its politics should serve as the "leaven" in human society; as citizens of heaven, we are not called to retreat but to engage responsibly as

37   John Vernon Taylor, *Christianity and Politics in Africa*, Greenwood Press, Publishers, Westport, Connecticut, 1957, pgs. 18 – 21.
38   George Ernest Wright, *The Biblical Doctrine of Man in Society*, SCM Press Ltd, London 1954, pg. 137.
39   Wright, 150.
40   Joseph Edward Fison, *The Christian Hope*, Longmans, Green and Co., London, 1954, pg. 50.
41   Fison, 50.

citizens of this world.[42] The Church in society must be different but involved. The Church, according to Taylor, must bring both judgment and creative participation to society. The Church serves in judgment as a prophetic voice; it engages and participates creatively by co-opting with the State in the promotion of welfare for citizens and removing economic and civil wrongs.[43] Taylor concludes that there are risks involved in responsibility. The arena of national politics in particular presents dangers and temptations of a subtle kind. Yet, he challenges, *someone* must stand in this place of spiritual danger. Who better, than the Christian?[44]

A core element of the Church's mission is one of justice. According to Gary Haugen, author of *Good News About Injustice*, injustice happens when power is misused to take from others what God has given them: life, dignity, liberty, the fruit of their love and labor.[45] As Christians, because the love of God is in us, we are all called to do something about injustice. The most crucial role, Haugen argues, lies with shepherds and teachers in the Body of Christ. Our leaders must teach us about our God of justice so that we can follow Him in the struggle against injustice.[46] Furthermore, our leaders need to lead by example in word and deed in this struggle. Guillebaud writes, "Had the church [and her leaders] not kept silent in the face of the assassinations which led up to the genocide, or the injustice for the forgotten refugees in Uganda who eventually invaded as the RPF, the horror of the Genocide may not have ever happened."[47] Furthermore, had the Church and her leaders listened to the cries of the Hutu suffering under forced labor and spoken out against such cruelty during Belgian rule, the cycle of injustice and pain would have been broken earlier.

Julius Nyerere, former President of Tanzania, speaks prophetically with a clarion call regarding the role of the Church. The Church, he says, sometimes must co-opt with the government and authorities to help the people. At other times the Church must work in opposition to those same powers and authorities. Always the Church must be on the side of social justice, helping people to live and

---

42   Taylor, 21, 27.

43   Taylor, 30 – 31.

44   Taylor, 34.

45   Gary Haugen, *Good News About Injustice*, InterVarsity Press, Downers Grove, Illinois, 1999, pg. 72.

46   Haugen, 175 - 176.

47   Guillebaud, 330.

work together for their common good.[48] William Temple, author of *Christianity and the Social Order*, concedes that when the Christian Church makes her voice heard concerning political and economic matters, resentment is often felt, even from Christians. He attributes this sentiment to the modern and "enlightened" idea that religion is only one department of life, like Art or Science. It is assumed that the Church exercises little influence and should exercise none.[49] Yet, regarding the important social issues of his day, Temple says that in the name of justice Christians cannot ignore such challenges. The Church has been commissioned to carry out the purposes of God. As the "Body of Christ" we are to be an instrument of His will. Thus, we are obliged to ask what the will of God is concerning every field of human activity. Finding God's purpose for every sphere of life is the role of the Church. If there has been deviation, the Church's role is to bring restoration. Thus, the Church "is bound to 'interfere'," argues Temple.[50]

Laurenti C. Magesa and other Developing World theologians and scholars such as Gustavo Gutierrez and Desmond Tutu, argue that the quest for justice is a "biblical mandate."[51] The Kingdom of God is one of justice. Thus, the duty of theology is to advance the "biblical mandate" of justice. While theologians who advocate for justice will be accused of "meddling in politics," they must be faithful to this calling and task, sharing Christ's ministry to bring good news to the poor and setting the oppressed free. This proclamation of the Gospel to the poor will not endear one to the unscrupulous politician. When positions of power are threatened, politicians will misinterpret the liberating work of the Church as "interference in politics." Politicians often understand politics as self-serving. Yet, the Church must speak prophetically against unwarranted domination over the helpless, the weak, and the exploited. Civil ruler's impunity and abuse of power must be challenged.[52]

Unfortunately, in Rwanda we find an example of the failure of the Church to embrace this prophetic call. Wolfgang Schonecke makes a credible critique of the Church in Rwanda, stipulating that despite countless acts of individual heroism, a Church that doesn't openly and honestly address its own ethnic tensions cannot speak to society with a united and trustworthy voice. Furthermore, regarding

---

48   Adrian Hastings, *African Christianity*, The Seabury Press, New York, 1976, pg. 86.
49   William Temple, *Christianity and the Social Order*, Penguin Books, Baltimore, 1942, pg. 13.
50   Temple, 24 – 25.
51   Magesa, 143.
52   Magesa, 143 – 145.

reconciliation, the Church cannot work effectively in this vein for the betterment of society until it addresses its own cultural and ethnic tension.[53] Tharcisse Gatwa recognizes that the Church as well as the whole of society in Rwanda have been victims of the genocide. Yet, he also suggests that Church failed to provide spiritual and moral guidance before and after independence in Rwanda. The church hierarchy either declined to see the misery and suffering of victims or blamed others for being responsible.[54] Churches not only refused to hear the cries of the victims of injustice, some even contributed in shaping policies and a model of society which was blatantly based upon discrimination. The true mission of the Church was in short supply as churches became allies to oppressive elites, silent to the call of God, and utterly blind to God's presence among the suffering.[55]

Yet, there is a way forward. The Church of Rwanda must consider the ways in which she needs to both confess and repent, renewing her covenant with God and recapturing a measure of trustworthiness. One practical way the Church can help the larger society recover its integrity is to address the fundamental question of a distorted history, a manufactured "Rwandese ideology," handed to them by the social Darwinist theories brought to them by Europeans in the late nineteenth and early twentieth centuries.

Secondly, the Church must also repent. According to Gatwa, some church leaders believe that because the church is "holy," only individuals ought to repent. For Christians, argues Gatwa, to desist from repentance is a denial of identity. Citing the tradition of apostolic succession in the Catholic Church, Gatwa alludes to a significant dimension in the life of Peter (the pillar of the church) - his repentance for denying Jesus. In fact, Peter became the pillar *because* of his repentance. Likewise, contends Gatwa, the future of Rwanda rests with those who repent of their guilt and cowardice. Confession of guilt and repentance are of paramount importance. Moreover, such repentance must take on a corporate nature. The Church of Rwanda must face up to its failures. Such repentance, although it will not absolve individual or corporate culpability, will pave the way for grace and healing, will open up communication, will establish new relationships and community, will eradicate evil, and will prevent the transmission of evil from this generation to the next.[56]

53   Schonecke, 3.
54   Gatwa, 359, 361.
55   Gatwa, 360.
56   Gatwa, 359, 361 – 362.

In conclusion, the Christian faith must govern "all of life" and can find its entry point in Rwanda through the social/economic/political aspirations of its people. While the East African Revival powerfully affected thousands upon thousands of lives in Rwanda, its major deficiency was that it did not emphasize the role of faith in the public/political arena. Christianity must be understood and prophetically lived out within its given political context. The Church's mission is one of justice. The Church of Rwanda has the opportunity to repent of her shame and failure, and now find her prophetic voice in all spheres of life.

www.ingramcontent.com/pod-product-compliance
Lightning Source LLC
Chambersburg PA
CBHW061745020426
42331CB00006B/1358